M000022275

ELVIS
After Life

ELVIS
After Life

*Unusual Psychic Experiences Surrounding
the Death of a Superstar*

Raymond A. Moody, Jr., M.D.

Peachtree Publishers, Ltd.

Published by
Peachtree Publishers, Ltd.
494 Armour Circle, N.E.
Atlanta, Georgia 30324

Manufactured in the United States of America

10 9 8 7 6 5 4 3 2 1

Library of Congress Catalog Card Number 87-61477

ISBN 0-934601-40-2

*Jacket illustration "Spirit of a King" by Sue Maylam,
Carrollton, Georgia*

Dedicated to the memory of
the King of rock 'n' roll.

Table of Contents

Introduction

On August 16, 1977, when he was forty-two years old, Elvis Aaron Presley died at Graceland — his home in Memphis, Tennessee. All over the United States and around the world, millions of people — the vast majority of whom had never even met him — were shocked and saddened when they heard the news.

During the decade now separating us from that event, the dimensions of the loss felt so deeply by so many on that day have become steadily more apparent. For, as will become clear in this book, as a people and as a culture, we can't let go of Elvis. He lives on and on in the thoughts and memories and dreams of his fans. He lives on, also, as the ostensible central figure of fascinating and occasionally baffling psychic experiences — reported paranormal events and mental states — which tantalize us, and which reveal, again and again, the depth of the affection which his fans hold for him.

Over the past nine years, I have gathered numerous cases of unusual psychic experiences involving Elvis Presley. (This research evolved from my work with near-death experiences.) I haven't yet made up my mind as to the ultimate "reality" of so-called psychic experiences, but this book is by no means an attempt to prove or to disprove the possibility of paranormal phenomena. As a doctor of medicine and a psychiatrist, I am intrigued by these accounts for quite a different reason. They interest me for what they reveal about the human mind and spirit. They tell us a lot, I believe, about the psychological aspects of what it means to be a devoted fan, about the nature of our relationships with celebrities, and about some of the less well-understood manifestations of the human process of mourning. For that reason, I think it would be a mistake to dwell on the sensational aspects of these touchingly human stories.

The case reports I have collected vary widely in kind and theme. Some are apparent "premonitions" of Elvis's death, others involve unusual behavior noted around the time of his death in objects that were somehow associated with him, a few are purported "apparitions" of him after his death, still others are unclassifiable. Although, as I said, I have no idea about the possible "reality" of such experiences, I am confident that the persons who were kind enough to relate their experiences to me were honestly describing the truth as they understood and interpreted it.

In what follows, the cases will be presented much as they were told to me during interviews, from which I have quoted liberally. I have edited the transcripts in such a way to make them more readable, *i.e.*, by placing the events in the narratives in correct temporal sequence when necessary, by tidying up grammar and sentence structure, and by minimizing the repetitions which are so common in spontaneous speech. Also, in order to protect the privacy of the individuals concerned, I have changed identifying details such as names, dates, and places. I have not changed the substance of the stories by these alterations, however.

I should add, in order to place this study in better perspective, that I liked Elvis Presley's music and performances from the time I first heard him, when I was eleven years old. Like countless members of my generation, I grew up listening to his records, and I, too, reacted personally to the news of his death. So my interest and involvement in this project are, in part, a manifestation of my own sense of loss and mourning for a unique and irreplaceable human being.

CHAPTER I

Forebodings

DREAMS WHICH SEEM TO foretell the deaths of loved ones, though uncanny and at times apparently inexplicable, are nonetheless a fairly common, and certainly very ancient, human experience. Elvis Presley was beloved by millions. I have been able to find four cases of persons who, shortly before or around the time of his death, had some kind of experience which, at least in retrospect, they took to be premonitions of his death. Extrapolating from these four instances, one can assume that a considerable number of his fans feel that they had some sort of forewarning of the tragic event.

The four stories which follow are in many ways typical of the kinds of experiences described by normal people who believe they "know" in advance that a loved one is going to die. What is atypical about them is that they involve the death of a well-known celebrity. We will consider later in what respects this difference makes them special.

Randy Graham is a clerk in a men's clothing store in Philadelphia, but he has always had a talent for singing and songwriting, too. His dream has always been to turn that gift into a career. Now he feels that he's getting a bit too old realistically to expect that to happen. He still enjoys music, though. Elvis is his favorite musician, a preference he shares with his wife, Lily. In 1977, before the two of them married, Randy had a particularly vivid dream which seemed to foretell the death of Elvis Presley.

66The date was August 15th, 1977. We were living then in California, which is where we met. Lily and I had been going together for more than five years. That was a rough time in our relationship. We had a quarrel and almost split. We went down to the beach to do some talking and cool down. It was at night, probably eight or nine P.M. I wanted to work things out but something told me it was hopeless. I wanted to get married, but Lily wasn't ready to make a commitment. I was discouraged and thought she would never settle down. Things were definitely on the downswing.

To tell you the truth, it was our mutual interest in Elvis that brought us together. That was the main thing we had in common at first. My admiration for him was stronger than hers, but she is a strong fan, too. Don't get me wrong. We don't spend all our time on this Elvis Presley kick. We saw three live concerts together, that's all. Once we went to a meeting of one of his fan clubs in California, to check it out. We never went back. That wasn't our crowd.

The night of August 15th we took our tape player and some Elvis tapes to the beach and lay down on a blanket. We talked things over. I was exhausted that night — too much work and too much tension between Lily and me. I remember looking up the beach to my right and seeing a couple walking down the beach toward us holding hands. They were probably a hundred feet away. I could see them in the light of a street light. Our Elvis tapes were playing.

I was trying to talk with Lily but I felt myself slipping away into a snooze. This dream started as soon as I dropped off to sleep. I dreamed that Lily and I were in an auditorium. For some reason, I concluded it was in Europe. It reminded me of a theater you might see in Europe. The curtains were made of some heavy, thick, lush material. They were maroon. The walls of this place were of dark-colored wood. The walls were carved with scenes from his life. I saw him as a young man with his mother and father; he was standing between them. Then there was a carved wood panel showing him performing. There was another of him marrying Priscilla. All these were carvings in the wood of this theater we were in. Lily and I were the only ones in the auditorium.

Suddenly the lights came on, like a very bright spotlight. The curtains parted a little and Elvis stepped out onto the stage. He was dressed much like you see him in old films of his early performances. He was holding a guitar. He looked at us and he said, "This is my last concert. Glad you could make it." This was as real as life. I heard his voice when he spoke. It was his voice, all right.

He started singing. First he sang "Can't Help Falling In Love With You," then "Loving You," then "I Gotta Know," then "It's Now Or Never," then "That's When Your Heartaches Begin." In that order. It was Elvis at his best. I heard every word clearly. I can't emphasize enough how real all this was. Now, I know at this point you're wondering if those were the songs that were playing on the tape recorder on the beach at that time, during my dream. No, they weren't. We didn't even have any of those tunes with us. Yet I heard every one of them like he was standing there singing them.

When he finished singing, he said, "Thank you very much, Lily and Randy." Then he went behind the curtains and I woke up. That dream was so real! I told the whole dream to Lily when I woke up. She said the whole time I was asleep I looked like my jaws were clinched and I was making a funny noise, like mumbling. The dream couldn't have been more than a few minutes long. She said I hadn't been asleep more than ten minutes. When I awoke I noticed that the couple I had seen to my right just before I went to sleep had walked past and were now down the beach to my left. So it couldn't have been long.

I told the whole dream to Lily. She got upset. She said, "Randy, why did you have a dream like that? That's terrible, Elvis saying, 'This is my last concert.'" It made Lily cry. I wondered why she was upset like that.

The next day I was at work. Lily called. She said, "Randy, Randy. That dream you had last night about Elvis's last concert. It came true. Elvis died today." She was wailing but I couldn't believe it. I thought it must be a joke. It's funny, but I don't even remember the next few hours. I have no idea what I did. I do remember I left work immediately and went to Lily's apartment. I don't remember anything after that until I woke up the next morning. Lily says I stayed at her place for a while and cried, then went off for a drive by myself. I'll never get over Elvis Presley dying. It seemed like the end of the world. I think I must have been tuned in to him that night. I don't know how but I think I picked up that he was going to die.

That night on the beach was important for Lily and me. We got a lot of things worked out. We married a year and a half later. Now we have two kids. **"**

After Randy finished telling me his story, I pointed out some things about the dream which intrigued me. I was interested that the dream had come in a troubled period in their relationship; it seemed to me that the dream had more to do with their relationship than with Elvis's death. They had been brought together, Randy said, by their interest in Elvis, and he was one of their chief common interests. I suggested that the figure of Elvis in the dream represented their relationship, and the theme of Elvis's career drawing to a close reflected Randy's fear that the relationship between Lily and him was about to end. Even the songs and the order in which they were performed in the dream (Randy was able to remember this, he told me, because he told the dream to Lily as soon as he woke up and then wrote down the dream) seemed to reflect the stages of their involvement, starting with the beginnings of love and continuing through to heartbreak. The themes of some of the latter songs also reflect Randy's concern about Lily's lack of commitment at that point — "I Gotta Know" and "It's Now Or Never."

Obviously, because of his uncertainty, he was giving Lily a kind of ultimatum: commitment or nothing.

Lily's reported reaction to the dream is consistent with this interpretation, too. She became anxious. Perhaps, I thought, she had sensed that the dream was connected with Randy's thoughts about breaking up. Obviously, both Randy and Lily see the dream otherwise. They believe that the dream was a glimpse into the future, a psychic connection with the death of a man they both loved.

Nora Wilson, a Connecticut woman, was fifty years old when Elvis died. She, too, is a long-time Elvis fan. She gives an account which is in certain respects similar to Randy Graham's.

66About three days before he died, I saw Elvis in a dream. He looked tired, tired and sad. In the dream, I wanted so much to comfort him or to do something for him. I reached out and touched him on the arm, and I said, "Oh, I feel so sorry for you. Isn't there anything I can do for you?" As tired as he was, he tried so hard to smile at me, but he was so exhausted and discouraged that his smile looked real weak. When he smiled, I thought to myself, "Well, we've all done it to him — all of his fans. We just wanted more from him than any person could give. I think we've hurt him very much. I wonder if he's going to die."

When I thought that, he seemed to look not quite so worried, and he said, "I feel that I am going to die. I worry about how my fans are going to take it. All those people, they love me and I love them." Then it seemed that Elvis started looking much younger, like he was melting off years until it looked like he was about thirty years old, I guess, happy and smiling. Then everything in the dream grew very bright, like you lit it up by turning on a bright light in a room.

Then a few days later I was sitting in front of the television set in my living room, and the news came on and they said that Elvis Presley had died. My sister was sitting there with me and when it came on she said, "Oh, no," and she started crying, just sobbing. But as for me, I thought, "Well, I knew it." I wasn't surprised, but still I was very sad. I thought, "Just like he said, we loved him and he loved us."

I was content in one way, because the way he had looked in that dream — so swollen up (swollen and sad and worried) — I think it would've been a relief to him to die, and the dream had seemed so real to me. But still I have never given Elvis up, I guess. I still miss him and wish he hadn't died. "

Nora's story is typical of a quite common type of dream: a dream in which someone experiences the death of a loved one. Nora lives alone and the only person who is very close to her is her sister, whom she sees once or twice a week. Even today, and even more so at the time of the dream, her love for Elvis provided her with a kind of substitute companionship which partly made up for her real-life loneliness. In dreaming of the death of Elvis, she was dreaming of the loss of a loved one.

Characteristically, people who have this type of dream report that they awaken in a gloomy mood, with feelings

Dr. Raymond Moody

of sadness. This is precisely what happened to Nora. She told me:

❝I was sad from the time I woke up, all three days before we heard about Elvis dying. Sometimes I would burst out crying. I would have to shut myself in my room, go to bed and cry. All this was even before Elvis died.**❞**

Like Randy Graham, Nora Wilson is of the opinion that her dream was a kind of magical foretelling of Elvis's death. She denies ever having had any other precognitive dreams or other uncanny experiences.

Lynn Harper, a young woman who is now a high-school athletic coach, also had an experience which appeared to foretell Elvis's death. Although she says she was never asleep during the episode, some kind of alteration in her state of consciousness was taking place.

❝I was lying in bed in my room on the morning that Elvis Presley died. It was about eight o'clock A.M. I knew that something was happening because I felt nauseated and nervous, but I didn't know of anything there was to be nervous about. I had never felt that way before. I was nineteen years old then, and I remember that at first I thought that I had an illness. I remember my hands sweating. My heart was beating fast.

Why, I don't know, but suddenly, just very abruptly, I started thinking about Elvis Presley. In my mind, I was

-8-

going over as much of his career as I had learned about in my lifetime up to then. I thought about what I had heard about his childhood, that he had been very poor. They say he got started as a singer when he was a very young boy. I remember thinking for a while about the influence he had had on some of the musicians that I had listened to as I was growing up.

At first, I wasn't seeing any of this in my mind's eye, if you know what I mean. It wasn't in the form of mental pictures, but just thoughts about Elvis. At a certain point, though, it turned into pictures, very plain ones. The first one was of Elvis and he looked pale and sick. There was not much background in that picture. He was in a plain-looking bedroom and the curtains were drawn so that there wasn't much light in there. That picture was just a flash, almost. I saw it for less than a second, probably. The next picture followed in about a second. That one was in great detail. Elvis was lying in a coffin, surrounded by flowers. He looked still and dead. There were a lot of people walking around the coffin and they were all dressed in dark clothing, mostly navy blue and black. One woman in the picture was walking kind of bent over and wearing a black veil. None of the people were crying. They were all too numb to know what to feel, it seemed. That picture seemed to last several seconds. Then words came. "Elvis Presley is dead and this is his funeral." It was strange to be seeing this. It was odd to be intruding. I wondered if Elvis Presley was dead in actuality, because this was not a dream and I was completely awake. Then that picture went away and immediately another one took its place. The color in this one was magnificent and the picture itself lingered, probably about five seconds. Elvis was in a green field. The color was a very beautiful shade of green. Elvis appeared to be about twenty-five years old. He was standing beside a woman I took to be his mother, perhaps, even though they seemed to be about the same age. There were many others there also. They were all very happy. There was a lot of talking going on. There was beautiful music, too, but no one appeared to be singing. The music was uplifting and it came from everywhere, wraparound sound. This seemed to be heaven, and a soft light filled up everything there. The presence of God was all around.

This ended abruptly, and I was dazed and groggy for about an hour afterwards. It was very peculiar because for this whole time I was feeling that I had seen all those pictures before even though I knew that in reality I had not. For two or three hours I was nervous. My mother said that I was pale and she commented on my lack of appetite. She said, "Are you worried about something?" I told her that I didn't know of anything I was worried about. I didn't tell her about the pictures, because I was afraid she would insist that I stay home from the swimming class that I was supposed to teach that evening. I told my mother that I had a headache, went back to bed and slept all that day, until about an hour before the class. When I got to the class my girlfriend, who taught the class with me, met me at the door of the gym and said, "Lynn, did you hear that Elvis Presley died?" I was stunned, and I lost control. My girlfriend was frightened. She said, "Lynn, why are you shaking?" We started the class a few minutes late, but we did teach it. For the whole time, I kept thinking about what had happened and wondering what it meant. I am still wondering about it. Nothing like that has ever happened to me before or since. 99

In a follow-up interview with Lynn about two months after the original one, she remarked that she had definitely become more religious after her experience. She stated that she seldom misses church on Sundays and that she spends at least two or three hours weekly reading the Bible. She attributes this increase in religiosity to her experience, saying that since it took place, she has been more curious about the Bible, God and Heaven. She has never had a recurrence of the unusual imagery.

Also in the later interview she added a detail which she had not mentioned previously.

66 This whole experience was goofy in that during it, time was all broken up and the order [in which] things were happening was hard to grasp. Time was mixed up. All the next day I had some little trouble keeping track of what time of day it was. I don't know how to explain it to you. 99

Lynn's experience is interesting not only for its content — namely, the theme of Elvis's death and funeral, which it appears to foretell — but also because her account strongly suggests that at the time Lynn was undergoing an attack of a little-known neurological disorder called temporal lobe epilepsy. This is a form of seizure which is manifested not by the spasmodic movements of the limbs associated with grand mal seizures, but rather with psychological phenomena much like Lynn describes. Attacks may begin with feelings of nausea and restlessness; they often include vivid images; sometimes the images are of memories of the person's life. Visions of intense light, disturbances in the sense of time, difficulties in putting the experience into words (so-called "ineffability"), and an increasing concern with religion are also often reported. All these features were present in Lynn's case.

Why her visions involved Elvis is a mystery. She claims that she was not particularly a fan of Elvis Presley's; although she did like his music, he was not one of her favorite singers. During my interview with her, I could not discover any particular reason why the image of Elvis would figure so prominently in her episode of temporal lobe epilepsy.

While the three experiences reported above took place in some altered state of consciousness — the first two during sleep and the third during an apparent seizure — Roby Underwood's paranormal awareness of Elvis's death came to him in a state of full waking alertness. Roby is an insurance company executive in Chicago. He admits that he is still puzzled about what happened to him on the afternoon of August 16, 1977. He was thirty-nine years old at the time.

&&I spent two hours in my office that morning talking to a client. I had been angry at him. I left for lunch an hour late and felt grumpy. I was walking along the street on my way back from lunch. I remember it well. I spotted an old friend of mine walking along the street ahead of me and just as I saw him the words came into my mind, "Elvis Presley must be dead." They came in with conviction. It seemed a certainty that he had died. I caught up with my friend and spoke with him for a moment. He is an old fishing buddy of mine. No connection between him and Elvis Presley. I didn't mention what had just happened to me.

When I got back to the office I kept staring out the window. I couldn't get any work done. A couple of hours later my secretary walks in and she was red-eyed from crying. She says, "Roby, Elvis Presley is dead." I said, "Yeah, I know. I'm sorry to hear about it." I didn't tell her how I knew. I let it pass.

I don't have the vaguest idea why this happened to me. I liked Elvis but compared to my wife I was not a fan. She is wild about Elvis Presley. 99

Again, there is no simple explanation for Roby's experience. One wonders whether he might have overheard someone on the street talking about the death without realizing it, and then misinterpreted information he had received from the outside world as an idea coming from within himself. However, as far as I can tell or Roby remembers, the thought occurred to him at a time before the news was broadcast by the media. Roby has not had any other uncanny experience, before or since.

The four encounters reported in this chapter constitute a puzzle. In one way, I suppose, they probably don't seem so strange. Elvis Presley had many millions of fans. It was widely known before his death that he had been quite ill; he had been in and out of the hospital. Surely, his fans must have sensed the gravity of his situation. It is not too surprising, then, that on any one day around that time, large numbers of his fans must have had worries that he might die soon. On one of those days, it happened. Those persons who had thought about the possibility that he would die shortly before took their experiences to be supernatural forewarnings, while persons who might have had similar dreams or thoughts months or years before would have dismissed or simply forgotten about them. Therefore, we can find no irrefutable evidence of precognition here in any of these occurrences.

What we can find is a manifestation of our deep human yearning for control. To believe that experiences like these constitute supernatural knowledge of the future is, in effect, to believe that we human beings have a say in our own fate. If we have had an apparent magical forewarning of a future event, then, when the event transpires, we may feel somehow less "out of control" in the situation than we would have felt otherwise. In the concluding chapter of this volume, I will come back to this point and carry it further.

CHAPTER II

Elvis Pays a Call

RESEARCH DONE OVER the past few years has revealed an intriguing fact: A large percentage of widows have experiences of "seeing" or communicating with their husbands within a year or so after the death. This phenomenon is also frequently reported among other relatives or close friends of deceased persons — bereaved parents may have brief glimpses of departed children, living siblings of recently deceased siblings, and so on. Although one must be very careful about what one infers from these experiences, there can be no doubt that they happen to psychologically normal people in the context of bereavement.

Elvis Presley was beloved by millions of people, many of whom — even though they may never have met him personally — were intensely involved with him on an emotional level. It is perhaps not so surprising, then, that a number of these persons would have experienced "apparitions" of Elvis. In this chapter, I will present three case reports of persons who believe that they "saw" Elvis Presley after his death. No doubt there are many others, unknown to me, who have undergone such encounters. One of the persons whose visions are described below was personally acquainted with Elvis Presley and one had seen him briefly when she was a child, while the others had never been in his presence. None of them appeared to be particularly devoted fans of the singer. Their actual experiences vary as widely as do their respective personalities.

Hilda Weaver is an unmarried clinical psychologist, now in her late thirties. She is well respected in her community and among her colleagues. She says that she is "conservative" and remarks that she had no interest in paranormal experiences until she had her own. Almost three months after his death, when she was twenty-eight years old, she was visited — she is convinced — by Elvis Presley.

❝I had met him once when I was a young child, about ten or twelve years old. I say "met." Actually what happened was he walked by me. He looked down at me, held up his hand in a wave, and said, "Hi, honey." I remember what a thrill that was. There I was a little kid and all of a sudden a man who I imagined was passionately desired by half of the women in humanity was actually talking to me in an affectionate way. What a thrill! Of course, my thoughts immediately turned to marriage. [Laughter] What a thought! I remember that for a couple of months, maybe a year afterward, I entertained a little fantasy. I thought, "What if Elvis would marry me when I grow up and would take me away and we would live happily ever after?" [Laughter] What a trip! It gives me the giggles even now thinking about it.

But that was the only time I ever saw him in person. And I was not that much of an Elvis fan, really. Up to the time I had this experience, I had only seen a couple of his movies. And I have several of his records — you saw my record collections. I have about half a dozen of his albums, I guess. I was never obsessed by Elvis the way so many people my age are, however. Never. I have always been a serious type. Always studying, always interested in my work, which as you know is psychology. I think you probably know I'm a serious type. You talked to my friends today. You could tell they know I'm very serious, and you can tell it yourself. Academics were my life, always in a book.

That's why it was so surprising to me when I was visited by Elvis Presley. Now, you have to realize, this came right out of the blue, in a context of absolutely no interest in things like ghosts or ESP. No, I had always been very narrow minded about the human mind. I thought that stuff was all imagination or suggestibility. Which is why [Laughter] I have never told any of my colleagues about this, and why I probably never will. They would judge me just like I judged everyone else — even my clients — who ever mentioned those kinds of experiences to me.

So, this is what happened, and you'd better believe it floored me. I was in my office, in the evening, doing some writing — writing an article for a professional journal. The article was eventually published, it turns out. I'd better not tell you which article or which journal because if they found out, they might get panicked and try to retract it. Wouldn't they be surprised to find out what went on while I was writing it?

At any rate, I was in my office, lost in thought, and it was November 17th, 1977. I know because one of the things I did after Elvis left was that I made a notation in green ink on my desk calendar on the space for that date. The notation was "EP dropped by!" And I still have the calendar, by the way.

There I was in my office, writing, and I looked up and Elvis Presley was sitting in the chair across from me, the comfortable tan chair my clients usually sit in. It is amazing what your mind will do in a situation like that. As I realized who he was, and I sensed the overwhelming kindness that just lingered in the atmosphere around the man, I could tell that he thought that all was not well with me. This was surprising. I remember, because at that time I thought I was on top of the world. A practicing psychologist, very effective, very smart, very unattached, beginning to be very well off financially, and living in an absolutely beautiful part of the world.

So I could tell that he was aware that something was wrong in my life, something that even I wasn't aware of, and that he was trying to be helpful to me. All that passed between us, instantaneously, with great warmth and empathy. I am amazed even now at the presence of mind I showed at this most awkward and unusual moment. Often, I begin with new clients by saying something like, "What can I help you with?" But as I looked into Elvis's big, kindly face, I asked, "What can you help me with?"

He smiled, he actually beamed, and he obviously appreciated the humor. I looked closely at him. He

looked quite young, about my same age at that time, I
would say. And happy . . . he looked happy.

As I was going through this, my critical faculties would
come in and I would stop to analyze in flashes. I
thought, "Can this be happening? Can this really be
happening?" But even then, I really know that my critical
faculties weren't messed up at all. I was using them just
as effectively as I ever have. As a matter of fact, deep
down I knew I was overusing them. It was crazy, in a
way, I thought to be using them to doubt the reality of
something I was seeing before my eyes. I say, seeing.
Actually it was a far more intense process than just
seeing. Oh, I could see Elvis. He was wearing a blue
garment of some kind, flowing, attractive, but I didn't
dwell on the garment. The process involved seeing him
but even more it involved being in tune with him, interacting and having a relationship, a friendship. I felt like a
student and a sister and a friend all at once.

He began to talk with me, to communicate. He said,
"Are you satisfied with your life, Missy?" "Missy" was a
name I was called by a few of my close relatives when I
was young, but no one had called me that for years,
since I had gone off to college. That question hit me like
the proverbial ton of bricks. It seemed to go to the very
center of me, and I said, "You're a better psychologist
than I am, and you've never been to school." As soon as
I made that remark, and even as the thought had come
to me, I felt embarrassed and ashamed of myself, as
though I had come across as condescending to him. But
he smiled, and he turned the whole thing around from
very awkward to completely warm and in tune, immediately, by the way he replied. He said, "I've been to the
best school." And from the way he said it, I knew imme-

diately he was right. After all, he had *died*, for heaven's sake! What was I doing feeling so smart just because there was a piece of paper on my wall? I suddenly realized that I was in a realm where my Ph.D. wasn't a very good credential anymore. I couldn't hide behind it anymore. Always before when someone was in that chair, I could be the Ph.D. and use that to hide behind, to keep from facing myself. But suddenly, here I was with a man who had died, and he was asking me whether there wasn't something in myself that I wasn't yet willing to face, that I didn't know about.

I said to him, "Am I satisfied with my life? Oh, me! You know something about me that I don't know, that I'm not facing, don't you?" or words to that effect. And he kept silent and still, and looked into my face, so kindly.

Then I began to cry, from deep within myself, and he understood immediately, and he said, "Hilda, you must open up your perspective on what you are doing with your life." Then we conversed for a while, much of it was very personal, stuff that I'm not comfortable with sharing with anyone else yet. And by the time it was over, I understood that there is much more to the mind and the spirit of the human being than I had allowed up to then, and that if I was going to be a full human being to the point where I could be helpful to others, I had to realize this and let it affect me fully from within, and allow myself the liberty to explore it to the utmost.

When this had sunk in very deeply within me, it became clear that he was going to leave, and also that I wouldn't be seeing him anymore while I am in this life. And I was fully prepared on one level for him to go, since I think we had gotten done what he was there to do — to open me up more to myself and others and life. But on another level it was as though I was holding on, that I had such affection for him that I could not let him go personally. At that point, there came into my mind something that had troubled me. Shortly after Elvis's death, I read in the newspapers that two young women who were standing around Elvis's house after he died — there to express their grief, I suppose — that these two younger women had been run over by a car and killed. I had been upset when I had read that. I had been more moved by that event than I had been by Elvis's death, since they were so young. That event came to my mind, then, when it became clear to me that Elvis was about to leave, and I expressed my sorrow about it to him and I had some concern, too, for how it would have affected him. He said, "I was deeply concerned about them, too. I was there to greet them and to be with them when they passed over into heaven." Immediately, my concern about these two young women was resolved, and again this man had touched me with his kindness. And with that, I instinctively bowed my head and put my hands together, like you would in a prayer. When I looked up again, he was gone. And I have never seen him again, and I've never had any dreams about him. Once in a while, I play his records and listen to them.

That's my experience. There were no cosmic messages, no profound truths, no learned papers with footnotes. It was all personal — very warm and very personal. Since then, I've been energized. I love everyone. You know, whatever this life is, we're all in it together. And there is a lot to it which is not in books. And none of my clients or colleagues know that I had this experience with Elvis Presley. And none of them ever will. It's too personal, you see. What I do hope they can see is the effect it's had on me. It helped me open up, to make me vibrantly alive to life. That's what I came out of this thing with. **"**

After Hilda described her experience to me, she and I had a long discussion. I shared with her my own impressions. Certain features of what happened to her, I said, were consistent with the possibility that the experience had arisen from Hilda's own unconscious mind, in that it clearly fulfilled certain emotional needs she had at the time, some of which she was apparently not fully aware. In the first place, by her own account, she had not openly mourned Elvis. Yet at some level she obviously needed to do so, since she had formed a kind of bond with him when he showed kindness to her when she was a youngster. The experience with Elvis in her office can be interpreted as a manifestation of that need to mourn him.

Secondly, she expressed her sadness and unease over the tragic deaths of the bereaved young women who were run over near Graceland. The interchange with the apparition of Elvis Presley in her office that day provided her with some consolation over that event. Thirdly, Hilda remarked how, prior to the encounter with the apparition, she had closed herself to the spiritual aspects of life. It is well known among psychiatrists how, when a person denies and closes off some important aspect of himself or herself, that aspect will somehow make itself known to the conscious mind of the person, more or less insistently. This may take the form of vivid dreams, or it may take the form of difficulties or patterns in interpersonal relationships, as, for example, when rigid and unemotional men marry flamboyant, expressive women, as if to live their emotional lives vicariously. Perhaps, I thought, Hilda's repressed spiritual yearnings rose to the surface in the form of her vision of Elvis which commanded her, in effect, to awaken to dimensions of herself in addition to the narrowly rational.

Finally, before that fateful day Hilda had always been serious-minded. She had denied herself the enjoyment of the simple pleasures of life; she seldom had fun. At some level, she must have yearned for such pleasure. Elvis Presley, on the other hand, had a reputation as a fast liver who delighted in movies, roller skating, horseback riding, and imaginative games. To some, Elvis was almost the image of a fun-loving life. It is reasonable, then, that the image of Elvis might arise from the deep recesses of Hilda's mind to express her longing for more enjoyment of life. At any rate, she says she began to allow herself more fun after her conversation with Elvis.

Hilda sat calmly, smiling warmly, while I summed up these possible interpretations. When I finished speaking, I noticed that — quite automatically — she took a deep breath. Gradually letting it out, she seemed to sink into a state of relaxation and looked into my eyes. I had the feeling she was penetrating me. It was as though she had suddenly placed herself into my perspective. Then she appeared to come back to herself, and in turn remarked on my response to her story. Her comments were so wise, perceptive and witty that I will quote them here in full.

66Raymond, you've spent years studying the unusual experiences of other people, yet you've never had one yourself. That must be frustrating. But look at me. I never had any interest in this stuff, but it happened to me. You seem envious, even angry at me. You need to search within yourself to get to the core of this defensiveness. You are kind of fearful in your approach to these things conventional thinking says can't happen. You need to open up other parts of your mind. You'll be happier if you do. **99**

I was amazed, and also touched, by what Hilda said. No doubt she had attuned herself to telltale inflections of my voice as I spoke, and to facial expressions of which I had been unaware. At any rate, as she had remarked on my feelings of irritation and envy, which had been only preconscious during the interview, they emerged fully into consciousness, and I realized that she was right.

My conversation with Hilda also dramatically brought to my attention a certain intrinsic limitation to the method of trying to explain away psychic experiences by simply giving an account of the psychological dynamics of the person who has the experience. For although it certainly seems possible in some cases to show how the features of the experience touch upon unresolved conflicts in the mind of the experiencer, it is just as true that certain features of the psychological "explanation" of an unusual experience may derive from, or otherwise reflect, unresolved conflicts in the mind of the explainer. Hence, if one is going to dismiss someone else's experience because it can be seen to reflect that experiencer's psychological hang-ups, one seems equally obliged to dismiss a person's attempt to explain away the experience, if that explanation can be seen to reflect the explainer's own psychological hang-ups.

Claude Buchanon characterizes himself as a "retired farmer," and then goes on to add that, really, "farmers never retire." He still stays busy taking care of the farm animals and growing vegetables on his rural Tennessee acreage. Claude, a feisty, almost ornery man, who seems about as practical-minded as they come, states that he has never had any interest in the subject of ghosts, or, in fact, in any other so-called paranormal phenomena. He does recall that when he was a small boy his grandmother described to him the ghost that she and other members of her family had seen in their home, but he can't remember many details. His concerns seem to be focused almost exclusively on the welfare of his farm and his family. That makes his story of seeing an apparition of Elvis seem even more intriguing.

66Now, Doc, nobody better say anything bad about that boy where I can hear them, or they're going to have me and a lot of people around here to answer to. That was one good man, and funny, too, when he wanted to be. Elvis came out here twice, and I think he would've liked to come out more, but security was a problem wherever he wanted to go. One time when I was strapped, Elvis helped me out. How he found out about it, I don't know. He slipped me some money and I got me a pick-up truck.

This one afternoon, it was the day Elvis died, I was up on top of the ridge out behind the house tending to one of my cows that had hurt herself. I looked down the slope, and I saw Elvis walking up the hill right toward me. He looked the same as he always did, except at first there was what looked like blue smoke or a fog around

him, just slight. He walked right up on me, almost, and
I said, "Elvis, what are you doing here, boy?" I couldn't
figure out how he got all the way around back without
me seeing him drive up from the county road.

He must've been ten feet away from me. I could see he
had a smile on his face. He said, "I've come to say good-
bye for a while, Claude."

Right about then I heard Thelma, my wife, yelling
"Claude!" and I looked down the other side of the ridge
where the house sits. I saw the screen door at the back of
the house fly open and Thelma came running outside
into the yard. At first, I thought there must be a fire in
the kitchen or something, she was running out so fast. I
couldn't make out what she was saying right then, but
finally I heard her say, "Elvis has died! It's on the radio."

So that's how it was. I'm not sure whether I heard
Thelma yell first or I saw Elvis first. They were about the
same time. It was like I could look down the back side of
the ridge and see Elvis walking up toward me and could
look down the front side of the ridge and see my wife
running out of the kitchen door. I looked back around to
say something to Elvis and he was gone.

I looked around in the bushes for Elvis for a minute. I
couldn't believe what was happening. One minute he
was there, the next he was gone. I collected myself for a
minute, then I ran down the hill to the house. Thelma
met me at the gate to the garden behind the house and
she was crying. I was out of breath.

I said, "Thelma, I saw Elvis walking up the ridge not
five minutes ago." We walked up there and I showed her
where he had been. Thelma believed me from the beginning. I've got a good wife, Doc, and her family believes
in these things. But I never have.

I didn't sleep for two nights after seeing Elvis up on the ridge. I am still wrestling with this thing. I wonder why he came to tell me good-bye. He liked me and yet I was not a good friend of his. I believe he would have liked to come out here more often than he did. I wonder if it was on his mind to come out here around the time he died. It grieved me that he was gone before I knew what was happening and got a chance to tell him good-bye. I would have liked to thank him for all he did for me. But then I wonder why it was he came to me and not his friends when he died. 99

I discussed Claude's experience at length with him in January, 1980. It was clear that Claude was convinced that he saw the spirit of Elvis Presley; the reality of his experience was not at issue for him, and he was puzzled only by why Elvis had chosen to visit him in particular at that moment. I told Claude that it occurred to me that possibly his experience was a kind of waking dream which had been triggered by hearing his wife below telling him that Elvis was dead. Perhaps, I thought, the waking dream represented an attempt by his unconscious mind to see his friend again and to deny the ultimate reality of Elvis's death. Claude replied that although he could not say which was first — seeing his wife run out of the door down below or seeing Elvis walking toward him — he was nonetheless quite positive that he had spotted Elvis on the hill *before* he heard Thelma say, "Elvis has died! It's on the radio." He is certain of this, he said, because he remembers that when he heard her say that, he thought, "Elvis can't be dead because he's up here on the hill with me."

Still, I thought, it was possible that when he first heard Thelma yelling, she was trying to tell him that Elvis was dead, and although he was unable consciously to hear her well enough to determine what she was saying, it had nonetheless registered unconsciously. In that case, the visible apparition of Elvis Presley could have been an attempt on the part of his mind to deny the unconscious knowledge that he had that Elvis had died. Also, the blue haze which Claude reported seeing around Elvis may be an indication that what Claude was experiencing did not involve normal, waking visual perception but, rather, an altered, possibly dream-like state of consciousness.

Despite speculation like this, however, it is impossible simply to explain away Claude's experience or others like it. What we are left with, in the end, is the fact that an obviously sane and stable man, not given to flights of fancy, experienced something that day which affected him so deeply that he was unable to sleep for two days and which left him still visibly moved as he told me the story more than two years later. The actual "facts" of Claude's experience now elude us, having become impossible to establish with certainty; the psychological meaning of the event lingers, continuing to haunt Claude and at the same time assuring him of a life hereafter.

Another interesting experience of this type was described to me by Karen McNair, a young woman who serves as the executive secretary and organizer of an organization of professionals in the field of psychology. Her encounter with Elvis came in the context of concern about her own direction in life.

❝I am from around Memphis, an hour away, and I knew how intense it was in Memphis in the fifties and sixties, with everyone in love with Elvis and so on. I felt it must have placed a tremendous burden on him, in a way. It was such a tragedy when he died. You could feel the shock waves.

A short time after his death I started working with a meditation teacher. She had grown up as a real Elvis lover. At that time I was also heavily into the Catholic church. During that time my meditation teacher and I would sit and we would express great concern about the thousands and thousands of people on this planet who we thought were holding Elvis down, because they couldn't let him go on. She and I, in our separate meditations, would try to cut some of those strings so he could go on. It was a big concern to me. I really used to worry about that.

Years later, in 1981, when he had been dead for four years, I was miles and miles away from Elvis Presley, as far as I was concerned. One night, when I was meditating, I had a candle lit and I was staring at that. It was very late at night and I was giving myself a lecture about the fact that I really needed to get my act together and figure out my life. I really needed at that time to lose weight and to become more responsible in the world. I needed to take better care of myself, especially my physical body, things like eating vegetables, laying off junk food. I was going through the entire gamut of my faults that night.

Suddenly, out of nowhere, I heard speaking to me, in the room, Elvis's voice. I saw him in my mind, and I heard his voice. And what I heard his voice say was, "You had better listen to that." His voice snapped at me like a cracking whip. I had been in a quiet, meditative frame of mind, and his voice zapped at me from out of nowhere. This was so surprising to me. **"**

I should point out that Karen is a fully functioning member of society, known and relied upon by her friends and colleagues as a stable person. She reports a happening which, though regarded in our society as somehow unusual, is very common. As we will see later, there are conditions under which visions of this type are, indeed, quite normal.

CHAPTER III

Encounter on the Road to Memphis

I FIRST HEARD OF Jack Matthews's amazing encounter with Elvis Presley from Bill Grady, the manager of an auto parts business in a sleepy little town in Alabama. I had gone there to lecture, and I had mentioned my interest in this topic casually during the presentation. Afterwards, Bill came up and in a helpful and engaging fashion mentioned that he knew of a story which might intrigue me. Bill said that an acquaintance of his, a long-haul truck driver named Jack Matthews, once claimed to have seen Elvis on a highway after Elvis's death and had even, he believed, claimed to have given the singer a ride. Bill wondered if perhaps I might be interested in talking with Jack, who lived about eighty miles away in another Alabama town. I replied that I certainly would be interested, and Bill invited me to drop by his store the next morning. We could find out how to get in touch with Jack from the address file in his shop, he said.

I arrived at the shop at nine o'clock A.M. the next day. Bill smiled from behind the big oak counter and, reaching out to hand me a slip of paper on which was printed Jack's address and phone number, he invited me to sit with him for a while and have a cup of coffee.

As we drank our coffee, Bill told me that he wasn't sure that Jack would talk to me, that he was a loner who pretty much kept to himself. Bill also told me that Jack had had some health problems lately — stomach and lung trouble, he said, from drinking and smoking too much — but that I might be able to get through to him if I mentioned to Jack that Bill had told me about him.

When I got back home, I immediately started trying to contact Jack by telephone. The next four weeks were a frustrating time as I attempted again and again, without any success, to reach him. I left several messages with his mother, but he never returned my calls. Finally I forgot about Jack, assuming that he wasn't comfortable with talking to me.

One morning about 8 A.M. as I was sitting in my office, the phone rang. A sleepy, somewhat hoarse voice said, "Dr. Moody, this is Jack Matthews." Delighted, I explained to Jack that I am a psychiatrist who has a special interest in unusual experiences concerning Elvis and that Bill Grady had outlined to me the strange tale that he had heard Jack tell. Would Jack be willing, I asked him, to meet me sometime and tell me what had happened to him? Jack wanted to know what I thought about such things, whether I was going to label him a "nut" or a "liar." I replied that in the course of my study I had met many psychologically normal people who had reported incredible happenings involving Elvis Presley and that although I had no idea whether these happenings were actually "real" or not, I was convinced that the people who had told them to me were being sincere with me.

Jack sighed an audible sigh of relief. He told me that he had wanted to tell his story to someone who would listen sympathetically. He agreed to talk to me sometime soon.

About three weeks later, I got another call from Jack. In about two days, he told me, he would be coming through Tennessee. He asked if I could meet him at a truck stop near a certain town. He would probably get there about five in the afternoon, or perhaps a little later, he said. I told him I would be there. He would recognize me, I told him, by my tape recorder and my brown jacket.

On the appointed day, I arrived at the truck stop at about 4:15 P.M. Five o'clock came, and then six, and then seven, and Jack didn't show up. I had almost decided to give up waiting when, about twenty minutes before eight, I saw a tall, thin, somewhat grizzled-looking trucker walk in the front door and look around nervously. When my eyes caught his across the room, he nodded and walked toward me. He wore blue jeans, a blue plaid flannel shirt and leather cowboy boots. I noticed that he was carrying a red plaid wool jacket draped over his right arm. He had about a two-days' growth of beard.

As he reached the booth where I was sitting, he spoke to me. "Sorry I'm late, Dr. Moody. Had some trouble on the road a hundred miles back, and it's been raining hard besides." I looked out the window at the rain that had been pouring down for about an hour.

Jack sat down and we ordered dinner. As we ate, we learned about each other. Jack told me from the beginning that he had been under treatment for alcoholism and that he had been in the hospital three times to dry out. It was working now and he hadn't had a drink for almost a year. He had the sunken, soulful eyes of an alcoholic, I thought to myself.

After dinner, he lit up a cigarette. I suggested we talk about his experience with Elvis Presley.

"This was back in 1980. The date was December 20th. I remember it exactly because not only did it shake me up so bad but also this was two days before my mother's birthday, which is December 22nd. It was real important for me to get back home to Alabama for my mother's birthday. I was hauling a load to Memphis from out west and I had been worrying that if something went wrong with the truck I might not make it home in time for her birthday. I planned to unload in Memphis on the 21st and to drive home that night. All the family was coming on her birthday, but we were going to be there by ourselves on Christmas Day.

I was worried about my mother because she had been in the hospital two months before with heart trouble, and I was afraid that this might be her last birthday. I still live at home with her. I was married for five years but my wife left me in 1978 and I have been living at home with my mother ever since.

Anyway, I was running behind that night and it was dark. It was about nine-thirty at night. I was about a hundred miles west of Memphis. I knew that road well and I was planning to go on into Memphis that night. Now, one strange thing about this to me was that I hardly ever have picked up hitchhikers. Once, about six years before, I had picked up a guy in Nevada, and he turned out to be crazy and started yelling at me. He pulled a knife on me, but I knocked it out of his hand and pushed him out of the cab onto the side of the road.

I am an independent trucker but since that time I don't pick up hitchhikers. You never can tell who's going to get in the truck with you these days when you stop to pick up a hitchhiker.

But that night of December 20th was different. I had stopped for fuel. I was nervous and I got out of the truck to walk around and stretch for a while to calm my nerves. I drank two cups of coffee. The lights around the station where I had stopped were bright floodlights, but this was out in the country and the other side of the road across from the station was dark. There were trees across the road, a clump of trees. I looked over there and I thought I saw a light in the woods. Not a light like a flashlight but more a patch of light, like a glow coming from in the woods.

I wondered what it was. I wondered at first if I was seeing a bright cloud through the trees, but I never could tell where the light was coming from. I stood there by the road gazing at that smudge of light and trying to focus my eyes on it. Then all of a sudden I saw a fellow walk sort of in front of the light. He walked along the other side of the road toward the highway. I noticed he was wearing an overcoat and was carrying a bundle under his arm.

I guessed he had been walking along the road and passed in front of the light, but I just guessed that because by the time I saw him he was walking along the road. He may have walked out of the woods for all I know. I really don't know where he came from. I was just guessing that he had been walking along the road before I saw him, but I really don't know.

When I first saw him I didn't see his legs. He was walking behind some low bushes and I just saw from his head down to his hips. Anyway, he seemed to notice me and walked out toward the street. As he did I walked on across the road. There was no traffic on that road at the time.

I got right up to him, almost to the other side of the road from the station and I said, "Where you headed?" I felt sort of sorry for him. Why, I don't know. He looked worried. I didn't think he heard me. I had been speaking quietly and he didn't answer, so I said it again, louder. "Where you headed?"

This time he looked at me and said, "Memphis."

I said, "Going to Memphis for the holidays?"

He said, "Yeah, I'm going home to see my momma and daddy."

I noticed that he had a Tennessee accent and a deep voice. I couldn't see his face well because he had a big hat or maybe a hood over his head. I wondered why he was walking along the road a hundred miles from Memphis, so I said, "How are you traveling?"

He said, "I'm going over to the highway to try to hitch a ride."

Then he walked on and went out of my sight down the road. I went back to the station, got in my truck and turned around and drove back toward the highway. Where the station was was maybe half a mile on that road off the highway and I hadn't gone a quarter of a mile until I saw him again, walking along beside the pavement on the left side of the road carrying that bundle under his arm.

Before I had a chance to think better of it I had stopped my truck on the road beside him. I opened up the window and leaned my head and shoulders out of the cab and I said, "I'm going to Memphis. I'll give you a ride."

He thanked me and crossed the road in front of the cab and got in, and I drove on and got back onto the highway for Memphis. As soon as he got in, I could tell he was a real polite man. He kept called me "sir." Every little thing was "Yes, sir" this or "No, sir" that. I thought this must be a real fine man with good upbringing.

Well, I was real tired for the rest of the run into Memphis, but with the coffee in me I stayed awake, and so my rider and I were batting the breeze. I don't remember what all we talked about. I remember there was some talk about music we both liked. He told me that he was looking forward to seeing his mother and father. I could tell he felt about his mother about like I feel about mine. I could tell they were real close, as my mother and I are. He told me he had some presents for his parents in the package he was carrying. He also told me that he had been a truck driver for a while and he knew a lot about cars. He said he had several Cadillacs, but I didn't believe him. I thought he was just a poor boy trying to look big. I just let that one go and didn't say anything else to him about it. I thought it was pretty weird that a man with several Cadillacs would be hitching a ride home from out in the middle of nowhere.

We got along real well, though. I told him that I had been having trouble with alcohol. He seemed very understanding and told me that he had had trouble with pain killers and sleeping pills, so he knew how I felt.

All this time, it had been dark in the cab so I hadn't gotten a real good look at his face. I can't say for sure how old he seemed to be. I assumed maybe thirty or thirty-five, maybe younger. I don't know.

A few miles outside of Memphis, though, it began to brighten up from all the lights along the road and I could see him better. I could tell he looked familiar. I was sure I had seen him before. I asked him where he wanted to be let off, and he told me the address, which was Elvis Presley Boulevard. He said that he would get off as close to there as I was going. I had never gotten around to introducing myself and I wanted to know who he was, too, so I said, "My name is Jack Matthews." I glanced over at him for a second.

Just as I looked at him, he turned toward me and looked straight into my eyes and he said, "I'm Elvis Presley, sir."

I froze and I was stiff as a board. Sweat popped out on my forehead and my palms and I couldn't talk. I sort of stammered and I said something like, "You've got to be kidding." The next mile or so I was scared and I couldn't say a word. I can't say how I was able to drive that truck in the state I was in.

It was Elvis Presley, all right. Or his ghost. He looked just like he did in his heyday. I was quaking in my boots.

Finally he said that he wanted to get out at a certain road and I stopped the truck. I had seen a ghost, and my heart was pounding.

I never had been to Graceland at that time, but about two weeks later I got up my nerve and I went back to Memphis and went over to Graceland. It was real close, it turned out, to the spot where I had let him off.

Well, that's my story. I wasn't drinking at the time this happened. I had been on the wagon for about a week when this happened, and I swear I hadn't touched a drop that night. I hadn't taken any kind of drugs at all. **"**

After Jack had finished telling his story, I spent another hour asking him questions. I wanted to know whether he had been an Elvis Presley fan before the night of December 20th, 1980. He replied that he had liked Elvis all right, but that he much preferred country music to rock 'n' roll. His favorite singers were Willie Nelson and Waylon Jennings, he told me.

I remarked to Jack that it had struck me as I had listened to him that there were several parallels between his own life and character and that of Elvis Presley. In the first place, it is well known that Elvis was very closely attached to his mother, and it was obvious that Jack had a very similar bond to his mother. Both of them had been truck drivers, both liked cars, both of them had been divorced, both of them had trouble with substance abuse. Also, it seemed significant to me that when Jack met up with the apparition of Elvis on that lonely country road, Elvis's expressed concern was the same as had been weighing heavily on Jack's mind just before the encounter, namely, getting home to his family for a reunion.

Jack listened thoughtfully as I spoke, and he said that he was surprised at the similarities and parallels that I had just pointed out, and that he hadn't thought of it in quite that way. He asked me if I knew any psychological or medical reason for what had happened to him that night.

"In all honesty, Jack," I answered, "I really don't know. But if you want me to tell you one possible explanation that comes to my mind, I will, as long as you understand that I'm not trying to dismiss your experience out of hand and that I am just telling you this explanation as a possibility, not as a certainty."

"Shoot," he said.

My mind raced back over what I had learned in medical school, in my subsequent residency training, and in practice about a condition which sometimes occurs in alcoholics when they abruptly stop drinking, as Jack had told me he did "about a week" before the bizarre incident on the road to Memphis. I began to speak slowly to the kind trucker who was sitting across the table from me.

"Jack," I asked, "have you ever heard of delirium tremens, the D.T.'s?"

"Yeah," he replied. "They told me about that every time I went into the hospital for alcoholism. It's where you see pink rats after you go off alcohol. I've never had it, but several of the fellows who were in the hospital with me did, and they told me about it, too."

I told him that sometimes, a few days after an alcoholic stops drinking suddenly, he will start to have vivid hallucinations. He will see things that aren't there. He will sweat, and he'll shake and tremble. People who are going through the D.T.'s aren't able to sleep and they are very restless and frightened at times.

Jack was paying close attention as I talked. I paused and watched him take a sip of his coffee and another puff of his cigarette.

"Several of those things that happen in D.T.'s were happening to you that night." I went on. "You told me that you were 'nervous' when you stopped at the station. You were obviously pretty restless then, too, and walking around. Later on, you said that you broke out in a sweat and that you were frozen with fear. All this happened about a week, you said, after you had stopped drinking."

I paused, and as I did Jack stared soberly and reflectively off into the distance. He appeared to be lost in thought. As we sat there in silence I began to wonder if it was even possible that a man undergoing active delirium tremens would nonetheless be able to drive a huge truck one hundred miles without incident, as Jack apparently had done. Just offhand, it seemed unlikely, yet as soon as I had put the question to myself I remembered something that had happened several years before which put my mind at more ease. One night, when I was working in the emergency room, a man — coincidentally, also a trucker — had come in severely ill with impending D.T.'s. He was an alcoholic, and he told me that he had been driving along the highway in his truck from another state when the hallucinations began. He began to hallucinate dead bodies and large, grotesque animals lying alongside and on the surface of the road. Even in this condition, however, he managed to make it all the way back home — a long distance — to come to the hospital in his own town for help. I had my answer: It *was* possible for a person who was undergoing alcohol withdrawal and hallucinations to maneuver a truck along the highway.

Jack interrupted my reverie; his words jolted me back to the reality of a booth in a restaurant in a truck stop in rural Tennessee.

"All that that you say is true, Dr. Moody," Jack said. "It's true. And I had the shakes real bad, too, that night. I didn't tell you because I had forgotten about it. Now I remember. I was shaking real bad that night."

"Well," I said, "the fact that you were shaking is even more evidence that you were going through alcohol withdrawal. It is possible that the experience of seeing Elvis was a hallucination, if you were going through D.T.'s."

"So I might have just imagined the whole thing?" Jack asked.

"Who knows?" I answered. "Maybe it was part real and part hallucination. Maybe there really was a hitchhiker who really rode with you for a hundred miles, and you just hallucinated the last part about him being Elvis Presley . . . like a dream."

Jack looked uncertain. "I don't know, Doc," he said.

"I don't know, either, Jack."

We both laughed.

By then it was getting late. Jack wanted to get farther down the road that night before stopping to sleep, and the rain had let up. I walked him out to his truck, where we shook hands and Jack turned and climbed into his truck. He rolled down the window and looked at me; a friendly grin covered his face. By now the engine of the truck was chugging and roaring.

"To think. That whole thing might have happened because of my drinking, he said, raising his voice against the noise of the engine.

"Yeah," I said. "It's possible. But there's another possibility, too."

"What's that, Dr. Moody?" he asked.

"Maybe you really did see the ghost of Elvis Presley!" I shouted.

We both laughed again, and I stood there watching as the big tractor-trailer truck, its lights flashing, pulled away into the cool Tennessee mountain night.

Although delirium (which results, in effect, from a chemical disturbance in the function of the brain) may well have entered into Jack's experience, we can hardly assume that it accounts for the whole picture. There must have been deep-seated psychological factors as well, which also helped shape the content and the emotional tone of his encounter with Elvis. This is illustrated by the story of Bess Carpenter, in whose case delirium also appears to have played a prominent role. Here, though, the emotional context of her vision, and the role it seemed to play in her life when it happened, were quite different.

It alarmed and saddened Bess when she learned, in 1979, that she was pregnant. She wasn't married and had no prospects. The man whose child she was carrying lived far away, and she had broken up with him. She had no intention of letting him know about her pregnancy. She never seriously considered having an abortion, and there was no one to support her emotionally during her pregnancy. Elvis Presley had been her idol since she was fourteen years old. In her moment of greatest despair, she feels, he was there to help her.

66When I found out about the pregnancy, I was horrified. I wanted to die, which was unthinkable because I had two kids from my marriage to raise. I wasn't about to leave them wondering about why their mother had committed suicide. When I told my parents, they freaked out. I'll never forget it. It was on a Sunday, after church. I thought I could catch them in a forgiving mood if I told them then. No soap.

I hope you understand that I wasn't myself then. I got a divorce in 1977, with two kids. For two years I was hell-bent on self-destruction. It was depression, I guess. Believe me, when you are depressed you can do anything. So I ran around with a guy who was a bad seed. When I found out I was pregnant, I worried about it for two months before I told my parents. By then it was too late to get an abortion, which I wouldn't have done anyway.

My parents couldn't fathom a thirty-four-year-old divorcée with two kids and a Christian upbringing getting pregnant out of wedlock. They disowned me and wouldn't have a thing to do with me. I was absolutely alone during this time, let me assure you.

Well, I have a thing about Elvis. He was my dream man from the time I was fourteen. At my fifteenth birthday party, my girlfriends gave me a cake that had "ELVIS and BESS" written in pink icing on the top of it. Our names were enclosed in a heart. I love Elvis. I don't mind telling you.

It nearly killed me when he died. My divorce had come through a month before and I was just beginning to cheer up. The way I heard about it wasn't the happiest circumstance, either. I was eating dinner in a bar and grill on my way home from work when it came on television. When the news came over the tube, the place fell into a hush. There were some groans and sobs. This one drunk guy sitting at the bar mumbled something about being glad that Elvis was gone, and three people were on him right away, calling him unprintable names. What a creep. I could have hit him myself and probably would have if those three other guys hadn't shoved him out of there fast. My mother always used to tell me that if you accomplish something worthwhile in life, there will always be people around who want to bring you down. They will criticize people who've done great things to try to get the attention off their own inadequacies. I guess this guy was a prime example.

Anyway, I cried about Elvis on and off for weeks. I still cry about it sometimes. I went to Memphis for the funeral. Loaded the kids in the car and drove all night to get there.

The saddest part of my pregnancy in 1979 was going to the obstetrician's office and seeing other women there with their husbands. Naturally, I read a lot about pregnancy. My last pregnancy had been eight years before. Some of these articles talked about natural childbirth, the role of the father in the delivery, and so on. That really upset me. I was a wreck. I wished there was someone like that to be there for me.

I remember the date of this experience about Elvis Presley exactly. Naturally, it was November 4th, 1979. That was the day Todd was born. It wasn't one of those middle of the night things. He was born in the afternoon: 2:15 P.M. I went into labor that morning. I called my neighbor, Pat, and she took me to the hospital. My parents had told me they didn't want anything to do with it, so I didn't call them. Then, the next day when they found out from Pat, they were upset. "Why didn't you call us?" they said. My mother took to the bed for a week, she was so upset I hadn't called. There's no accounting for people.

When they wheeled me into the delivery room, they put this mask on me and I breathed the anesthetic. I was conscious the whole time, but I had a weird experience. The doctors and nurses were all around me in these white gowns, looking at me. Right there among them, Elvis Presley appeared. He smiled and winked at me. He said, "Relax, Bess, it's O.K. I'll be here with you." It looked just like him. I stared into his face, then I would blink or look away, but when I looked back he was still there. The others had on surgical masks but Elvis didn't. It was his voice, too. I'm certain of it. When you hear Elvis Presley's voice speaking to you, there can't be any doubt whose voice it is.

I stared into his face the whole time. He was so sweet. He stood there the whole time. Then, when the baby came, it was he who said, "It's a boy!" For an Elvis Presley fan, there can't be a bigger thrill than hearing Elvis himself telling you you have a new baby.

All the commotion started then. Doctors and nurses were running here and there, checking the baby and sewing me up and I sort of lost Elvis in the crowd. I didn't see him anymore after that. They wheeled me out of the delivery room and I tried to tell my doctor that Elvis had been there with me. The doctor didn't say anything but the nurses chuckled and said I was dreaming. But I wasn't dreaming. It wasn't like a dream. I'm not sure it was real, either. I still wonder what it was. Was Elvis there with me in the delivery room, or wasn't he? Whatever, I feel like he came through for me when I was feeling so low. I don't know for sure if it was real or not. I guess when I meet him in Heaven, I'll ask him and find out for sure. For now, I don't know. It's really like something he would do, no matter how it turns out. Either way, I appreciate Elvis. **99**

The simplest explanation for Bess's experience is that it resulted psychologically from her deep yearning to have someone there to support and to be with her during a particularly troubled time in her life. Her parents had turned away from her, and she had no husband, so she turned to an important figure in her life: Elvis Presley. Because she was delirious due to the effects of the anesthetic, she hallucinated Elvis. Whatever the actual mechanism of what happened, however, her experience had a positive emotional effect on her. What would have otherwise been a dreary episode in her life was turned into an occasion of joy and hope.

CHAPTER IV

"Here Comes Elvis": The Story of Jennifer

IT MAY BE HARD for others to believe, but Sherry and Jimmy Reed are convinced that Elvis Presley reached out from the hereafter to touch their little daughter's heart in the closing moments of her life, and they will be eternally grateful to him for it. Sherry and Jimmy were both sixth graders when the Elvis era dawned in 1956, and both have been fans for almost that long. Sherry was an unabashed admirer of Elvis from the first time she heard him.

&&I remember it like it was yesterday. I was in the sixth grade, and my friend Susan Logan was having me and several other girls over to her house for a spend-the-night party. Susan was playing some records on her record player, some Perry Como ones and some by Tennessee Ernie Ford, I believe, that belonged to her parents, and then she got one out of her drawer and she said, "Have you heard Elvis Presley yet?" None of us had and she played "Blue Suede Shoes." It was just terrific, of course, and we must have played it ten or fifteen more times that night until Susan's mother and father came in and told us we had to be quiet and go to bed. For the rest of my life, since that night, I have liked Elvis Presley. 99

In contrast to his wife, however, it took Jimmy quite a while to be able to admit his affection for Elvis.

66On the last day of school when I was in the sixth grade, we had a class party and we kids could bring records from home to play. Several of the kids brought Elvis Presley records that day, and I remember being very impressed by his music. I had never heard anything like that. But several of the boys said they didn't like it and so I went along with the guys because I didn't want to seem different. You know, it wasn't the thing for guys to like Elvis at that time because, let's face it, we were envious. I remember being very envious of Elvis over the next few years as I was going into junior high and then high school. So I had to act like I didn't like Elvis, as all the guys did, because although we all secretly liked him and wished we could be like him, you couldn't let on. That wasn't cool. We all envied Elvis, I'm sure. I know I did. I was envious of the attention the girls gave him, so I teased them about Elvis, just like the other guys in my group. But, in secret, of course, yes, I did like Elvis from the very beginning. I grew up with his music, after all. Later on, when I got into my early twenties, well, then I got over that envy and could enjoy Elvis in public, just like everyone else. 99

Sherry and Jimmy married in 1968, when they were twenty-three years old, in a little country Baptist church Sherry's family had attended for four generations. Jimmy was just starting out in his career selling life insurance, and Sherry stayed home in the little house that Jimmy's parents had helped them buy. They wanted to start their family right away. Even though the Beatles were all the rage at that time, Sherry and Jimmy played mostly Elvis records on the fine new stereo that Sherry's aunt had given them as a wedding present.

Almost two years after they were married, their daughter, Jennifer, was born, and immediately Sherry and Jimmy received a devastating blow. Their doctor told them that their little girl had Down's syndrome and would be retarded. Sherry vividly recalls the nightmarish feelings she had for the first few weeks of Jennifer's life.

66In a way, it felt like the end of the world. I had all these daydreams about what my baby would be like. I had hopes that my baby would grow up to be tops in everything — tops in looks, tops in personality, tops in sports, tops in school. I was awake when Jennifer was born. They gave me a spinal and I was awake for the whole thing. When Dr. Brown said, "It's a girl!" I was overjoyed, though I would have been overjoyed if it had been a boy, too.

I felt so happy. Yet just a few minutes later I knew something was wrong. I had known kindly old Dr.

Brown all my life and I could tell before he spoke something was wrong. At first he just told me that Jennifer wasn't doing well and he was going to call in another doctor. Then they brought Jimmy in and they told us about Jennifer's condition. I had heard of mongoloids before, and all it meant to me was retarded. I cried and cried. My daughter was going to be retarded. Jimmy was in shock, I guess. He didn't cry and he didn't say a word.

For the next few days, I cried. I loved Jennifer so much, more than I can tell you. I cried because I loved her and I knew she would miss out on so much because she was retarded, and I cried because I felt guilty. I just knew it was something I had done. In my mind I went over and over every little thing I had done and every little sickness I had during my pregnancy. I felt sure I had caused it in some way.

Dr. Brown and the other doctor kept on telling me it wasn't my fault. They said it was unusual for a woman my age to have a mongoloid child because mostly it is older women who have them, but that there was nothing wrong with my chromosomes. They told me it didn't mean I would have a mongoloid child the next time, but at that time for me there was not going to be any next time. I thought I would never risk facing something like that again. You just don't know the feelings the parents of a retarded child go through.

So I cried for a week and then it got worse. They told us they had found out Jennifer had a hole in her heart and that she probably wouldn't live to be very old. They couldn't give us any idea of how long she would live. She might die tomorrow or she might die in twelve years. They didn't know. It was horrible.

So we adapted. That's all you can do. We took Jennifer home and we took care of her. That child was a bundle of love from the beginning. She appreciated whatever you did for her and she would break out in the biggest smile. She was very slow in talking but she talked more and better than I had imagined was possible. As soon as her hair came out, it came out in beautiful blonde ringlets. She was a beautiful child.

When she was three we got her a puppy, a golden cocker spaniel. She named it Bup. Did those two ever love each other. Some days when it was raining and we couldn't go outside, they would chase each other around the house all day.

Naturally, Jennifer loved Elvis. We played Elvis records all the time for her and we sang his songs for her. The first time she saw him perform, I think, was on his TV special from Hawaii, and she smiled and laughed and danced the whole way through. She would watch Elvis movies on TV and I would show her pictures of Elvis from magazines.

She even got to see him in person once. Jimmy and I went to four of Elvis's concerts. Once we flew to Las Vegas to see his show there. When he came to our city when Jennifer was five years old, we took her with us to his concert. It was sold out, needless to say, but we had good seats. Jennifer was overjoyed. She squealed and screeched along with everyone else in the audience when Elvis came on stage. She talked about that evening for the rest of her life. She would tell everyone she met, "I saw Elvis!"

I don't think Jennifer ever had any idea about death. When Elvis died, naturally I felt terrible. I started crying when I heard about it across the fence in the back yard.

Our neighbor was hanging out clothes. I went out there to play with Jennifer and Bup in the yard and our neighbor told me that Elvis had had a heart attack and was dead. I let out a wail and cried.

Jennifer was upset that Jimmy and I were sad, but I don't think she fully realized that Elvis was dead and that we wouldn't ever be seeing him again. She went right on listening to his records and seeing the reruns of his television shows, so to her how would it be that Elvis was gone?

Jennifer had several hospitalizations in her life. She had three or four bouts with pneumonia. She was easy to get infections — why, I don't know — and she had a weak heart. In 1980 she got real sick and turned blue. Jimmy and I knew she was dying. Tears were streaming down our faces as we were taking her to the hospital, and she was saying, "Don't cry, Mommy. Don't cry, Dimmy." (That was her name for Jimmy.) She was so sick and yet she was concerned mainly for us. She didn't want us to be sad.

When we got to the emergency room, they took Jennifer into the pediatrics ward right away. Her doctor came and when he took one look at her, he knew she was dying. The next few hours were just a blur to me. They got Jennifer stabilized and for a couple of hours we hoped she might make it. We stayed right there in the room with her the whole time. The doctor and nurses didn't say a thing about us being there. They let us be.

As Jennifer was dying, she seemed to light up. The light looked as though it were coming from within her. She smiled a big smile. Jimmy and I were hugging her and crying and she tried to sit up in bed. She said, "Love you, Mommy and Dimmy." Then she said, "Here comes

Elvis." She was looking upwards and holding her arms out like she was trying to reach toward someone and hug them. She said it twice, "Here comes Elvis." Then she collapsed and died. She had the most beautiful smile on her face as she died, like an angel. She saw Elvis when she died. How nice. Just like him, isn't it? He was always doing nice things for people while he was here with us, and I guess he is still doing nice things for people where he is now, too. He was there to meet our little retarded daughter when she died, and she let us see that she was going to go on living, too. Never again since that night have I had any fear of death. I'll always love Elvis for what he did for Jennifer.

On the way to the hospital in the car, as I was holding Jennifer so tightly in my arms, I was so worried about what would happen to her when she died. I had always had a feeling that there must be a life after this one, but I wondered who would be there for her to take care of her. All her grandparents and aunts and uncles and cousins were still alive — no one she had ever been close to, I thought, had died. Then, when she died there in the hospital, Elvis came to meet her and help her as she died. Just think of it. God has such a perfect plan!**"**

Jimmy confirms every detail of Sherry's account of Jennifer's death. What he witnessed in that hospital room that night has changed his life forever.

"I was never a religious man before that night. I vaguely believed in God, but it was always something I put off thinking about. When I saw Jennifer smile and reach up for Elvis, though, I became a changed man. God is real, Dr. Moody. Anybody who could have seen my daughter's face that night would know it. In my moment of greatest desperation, when my only child was dying, and when I was expecting her death to be an awful, painful catastrophe to her and to Sherry and me, too, God came through and He sent Elvis, who she loved like she did Sherry and me, to help her and to make her happy.

Oh, some people will think we are touched in the head, I know that. But it doesn't matter what they say. They'll find out soon enough. That evening was the saddest and the happiest time of my life. Jennifer died, but I know she's alive with the Lord. And Elvis Presley came to meet her, and I got to see it all with my own eyes!"

The experience which Jennifer was apparently having while she lay dying is an example of what has come to be called a "near-death experience." In the latter part of 1975, newspapers, magazines and television programs all over the world reported that medical doctors in the United States had begun to study the experiences of persons who had "returned from the dead," that is, whose hearts had stopped beating when they were seriously ill but who had been resuscitated by modern medical techniques and who had lived to tell what it was like to almost die. Remarkably, most of these patients had described quite similar experiences, and — more remarkable still — the patients had been convinced by what had happened to them during their ordeals that there is a life after death.

In my book *Life After Life*, which was based on the experiences of 150 persons who had been to the brink of death and returned, I described the basic "near-death experience." The persons I interviewed described how, at the time their doctors believed they had "died," they felt themselves float up above their bodies and watch as the doctors and nurses below tried frantically to revive them. Then they felt that they entered into a dark, narrow tunnel. At the end of the tunnel, they came out into warm, beautiful, loving light. Many reported actually being met by relatives and friends of theirs who had died some time before. Some described seeing their whole lives pass before them in a review of bright, full-color images of the highlights of their lives. They often said that the experience was so peaceful and joyful that they did not wish to return, but were told that they had to go back to complete their lives in the world. When they did come back, they said that they were changed forever and that from then on they wanted to learn how to be more loving people.

Since *Life After Life* was published, many other psychiatrists, medical doctors, and psychologists have written books and articles confirming its findings. In fact, the Gallup Poll published a study showing that over eight million American adults had had experiences of this type.

In 1980, I interviewed a forty-five-year-old woman, Beverly Wilkins, who had had an experience of exactly this type. What happened to Beverly is relevant to my study for a simple reason: While Beverly was "dead," she claims, she met Elvis Presley.

Beverly has had a long career as a grammar school teacher in a small town in Nebraska. She is married to a prominent local banker and has two grown children. She is loved and admired in her community and has always been a stable and responsible citizen. When I went to interview her about her near-death experience — which I was interested in — I had no idea that she would be telling me about an after-death encounter with Elvis Presley.

I had arranged to meet Beverly at 3:30 on a Friday afternoon in April, just after school had been dismissed. As I entered her classroom, I found her still straightening up the room; the children had all left. She was a short, stout woman with a lively, friendly manner and sparkling brown eyes. She was wearing a light blue dress and had her dark brown hair arranged in a bun at the top of her head. She shook my hand and said she was happy to see me. We both sat down and chatted about her work in education and her deep, heartfelt convictions about the importance of good primary school education for young children. Then she began to tell me about what had happened to her the day her doctor thought she had died.

66In May of 1979, about one o'clock in the afternoon, I began to feel a pain or a pressure in my stomach, on the right side. I felt full and bloated but I wasn't nauseated. I assumed it was just indigestion and although I was hurting badly, I was teaching at that time and didn't want to alarm the children, so I just ignored it at first. But then it began to hurt in my back, too, so I left the children at their desks and went down to the principal's office. I said to him, "Mr. Walpole, I'm not feeling well." He took one look at me and said that he thought I had better go to the hospital. We made arrangements for another teacher to watch over my class, and Mr. Walpole took me to the hospital.

When we got there my doctor came and I was in terrible pain. At first they thought it was my kidneys, but then they did some x-rays and found out that it was my gall bladder. It was full of stones. They said I really should have the surgery right away because otherwise I could have another attack, and let me tell you, that was so fierce I didn't want to take a chance on anything like that hitting me again.

So three days later I had the surgery. They tell me that my heart stopped beating during the surgery and that I had no blood pressure. Why, I don't know. The doctor said he gave me up for dead, but another doctor tried shocking my heart and so I came out of it.

What I remember is this. Suddenly, I was awake and I felt so relaxed and happy I thought the surgery was over. I was wondering why I felt no pain. As I looked around I found I was rising up above the operating table. As I went up, I passed right by my doctor's face, and he had this look of fright on his face. There was sweat all over his forehead.

I saw that the nurses were pale and people were saying that I was dead. For my part, though, I thought they were being silly to be so concerned that I was dead. I felt fine. I looked down and I could see my own body on the table with that big gash in my side all sewn up. I wasn't concerned about the body at all, I felt so free. I knew they all thought I was dead, and I assumed I was, too, and for a moment I felt concern for my husband and children. I wondered what they would do without me, but as soon as I thought that, I stopped worrying because I knew the Lord would take care of them, as He always had. Just then I saw some other doctors and nurses running through the door with some medical equipment — I couldn't tell what it was, but I learned later that the heart shocking machine in the operating room wasn't working exactly right, so they brought in another one.

Anyway, suddenly I entered into a dark, round tube or hole. I could call it a tunnel. I seemed to go head first through this thing and before I knew it I was coming out into this beautiful, white light. The whole place I found myself in was filled up with love. It seemed to come from a source off in the distance. The place seemed holy. I could see beautiful scenes. Plants so beautiful and colorful you have never seen the likes of them here. It was like a meadow, with flowers and laughter and happy people all around.

As I walked through this meadow, I saw that the people were in little bunches, and one little bunch separated off from the others and began to walk over toward me. One was my father, who had died about two years before. He was radiant. He looked happier than I had ever seen him and much younger than he was when he had died. My grandmothers and grandfathers who had died were there to meet me, too, and it was the same way with them. Everybody was happy to see me, but my father told me that it was not my time to be over there yet, that I had some years to live before I died. They told me that I would be going back.

By that time, I was happy to be in that beautiful place, so I was disappointed to be told that I would have to return to my life. I was also relieved, though, that I would be allowed to go back to be with my children and Mel, my husband.

Just as I was getting ready to go back, and was feeling myself being drawn back, I caught sight of Elvis Presley. He was in this place of intense, bright white light too. He just came over to me and put his hand softly in mine and he said, "Hi, Beverly, remember me?"

Many years before, when he was giving a concert near where we were living at the time, I had met him briefly and we had had a short conversation. We really hit it off well and I think he really liked me because I just talked to him as a person, just like I would anyone else. I had liked him immediately, and I think he really appreciated it that I treated him just like any other human being.

Anyway, in this time while they thought I was dead, I saw Elvis in the light. When he greeted me, I said, "Yes, Elvis, I do remember you, of course. And many other people all over our world still remember and love you, too."

I hope you understand that although I am saying all this in words, in fact, in that place of light where I was, there are no words as we have them here. Everything that comes into your heart that you want others to understand is understood immediately.

So with this little interchange between Elvis and me, Elvis sort of receded into the light and suddenly my father was there with me again and was gently telling me that I had to go back to finish my life and that I would come again to that beautiful place when I died.

So I felt myself being drawn backwards rapidly and the light receded and then I felt a pop and I knew I was back in my body and that I would live. That experience changed my life completely. From that day forward, I have not feared death, because I know where we go when we die. I will also always feel blessed because I had that chance to be with my grandparents and my father again, and with my old friend, Elvis Presley. 99

When I initially interviewed Beverly, I had not yet conceived the idea of collecting what were then only a few disconnected accounts of psychic experiences involving Elvis and other celebrities into a book. So I didn't discuss with her the fact that Elvis had put in an appearance in her near-death experience. It had surprised me quite a bit, I confess, and even seemed to be unlikely. But, who knows? If Elvis Presley had been emotionally significant to her in life, there is no reason to think he wouldn't be emotionally significant to her in death, too.

Three years later, when I was beginning to put together my observations about psychic experiences involving Elvis, it seemed appropriate to pursue that thread in her experience. Accordingly, I called her and requested that she tell me in more detail about what had transpired between her and Elvis on that day in May, 1979.

❝Well, you know, he looked much like he did in this life, the way we saw him here. There were some differences though. He seemed filled with light, almost transparent to our way of thinking. So were the others I saw there. And Elvis looked younger than when he died. Very vibrant. I don't know what else to say. All of it is so indescribable. If you haven't had an experience like this, it sounds so strange, I know, but if you have it, it is the most natural thing in the world. Just wait and see.**❞**

CHAPTER V

Mysterious Meltings, a Falling Statue, and a Haunted Jacket

THREE OF THE UNUSUAL experiences I have gathered involve odd behavior on the part of inanimate physical objects which were somehow associated with Elvis Presley. All of the strange effects on objects reported here took place — or at least were observed — around the time of Elvis's death. Although each case rests entirely on the testimony of the individuals involved as to what they observed, it is quite interesting that the events appear to have a common pattern. I report them here just as they were related to me when I investigated them and have added some of my own impressions as to possible explanations of the various phenomena described.

In the fall of 1981, when I talked with her in the Kentucky city where she lives, Ruth Ann Bennett was forty-seven years old. Ruth Ann had been married for seven years when she was in her twenties, but she and her husband had divorced in 1962. One of the many reasons for the divorce, she stated, was that her husband could not tolerate her great devotion to Elvis Presley. Ruth Ann has never remarried. In the years since the divorce, she had worked as a waitress and manager in the restaurant she co-owns with a friend.

66Nellie Carr has been my best friend since junior high school. She is just as big an Elvis fan as I am. We have driven and flown over a lot of the country to see Elvis. We first saw him on stage in Florida in 1956. We drove all the way down there from Lexington and stayed with an aunt of mine. Elvis was unbelievable. You would not believe it if you ever saw him on stage. The crowd screamed the whole time, us included. I have touched him in crowds three different times and one time he actually kissed Nellie. That was in Memphis.

I will never forget the day Elvis died. I was waiting on tables at the restaurant. It had been a busy day. The telephone behind the cashier's desk rang and my partner answered it and said Nellie wanted to speak to me. I was kind of annoyed that Nellie would call me at work at such a busy time. When I picked up the phone and heard her voice, she was crying. She sounded so weak I thought she was sick. When she talked I remember it felt like a lightning bolt had gone through me. I guess she said, "Elvis is dead," but I was so shocked I couldn't hear it. It didn't sink in. I had to get her to repeat it three or four times. I kept saying, "What did you say?" Finally my partner looked worried about me. She came over and took the phone from my hand and said, "Nellie, what is it?" Then my partner said, "Oh, no," and she put the phone down. She started crying, and by this time it had sunk in with me and I started crying, too.

We were standing in a little storage area, almost a closet, behind the cashier's desk. It's funny. I have known my partner, Lois, for a long time and she never seemed to like Elvis Presley particularly. She would never talk with Nellie and me about Elvis. Yet, when Elvis died, there she was crying as loud as we were. Lois and I wondered what we should do. There were several customers in the restaurant at that time and we didn't want to upset them during their meals.

I was waiting on this one table with two men and a woman. They were northerners. I went out to take them their pie for dessert. When I went out there I knew they could tell I had been crying. My eyes were red. I couldn't contain myself anymore. I said, "I am sorry. I am upset because Elvis Presley has just died." The woman started sobbing and the two men were upset, too. They seemed sad, but they didn't cry. None of them ate another bite of the food.

The rest of the day was terrible. I didn't want to leave Lois to do all the work. Besides, she was upset, too. So I stayed for the rest of the day in the restaurant. We turned the radio on in the kitchen and I would listen to it when things were slow. By then all the radio stations were talking about Elvis.

At ten o'clock that night Nellie picked me up at the restaurant and we drove over to my house. We were going to watch the television reports and talk about Elvis and play my Elvis records. I kept my records in a big, built-in wooden cabinet along the wall in the den. I had kept the records in there for eight years, ever since I moved into this house.

I had never had any trouble at all with my records as long as I had them in there. I had last played them two weeks before. I remember because it was the night before I had gone away on vacation. I had been gone to the beach for ten days. The records were all fine then.

Anyway, that night when Nellie and I got the records out to play them, half of them were melted and warped so much you couldn't play them. Some of them were still warm to the touch. Immediately, I connected it with Elvis dying. I don't know how, but I am sure they are connected in some way.

Nellie was more upset than I was. She said, "Ruth Ann, this is weird." We stayed up for the rest of the night talking about it. Why in the world would my Elvis records melt on the day he died? 99

Ruth Ann showed me the wooden cabinet in which she had stored her record collection until the night of August 16th, 1977. She moved all her Elvis memorabilia out of the cabinet that night. She told me that she had kept the records on the bottom shelf of the cabinet. There were two upper shelves in the cabinet, and she had kept her Elvis scrapbook, pictures and posters there, she said. None of the other material had been damaged in the incident, she told me, with the possible exception of two Elvis posters which had been scorched brown around the edges. She could not be sure, however, whether they had been that way before the night of August 16th.

I asked her whether the records might have been damaged while she had been on vacation and the house had been shut up. She replied that she had left the house shut up in the summer many times before, for periods as long as two weeks, and had never had any trouble with items in the closet being damaged. I asked whether there had been any electrical equipment or flammable materials in the closet which might have overheated or ignited, and she said there was not. It even occurred to me that she might have been the victim of a cruel practical joke. I asked whether she had any acquaintances who might have sneaked into her house that day while she was at work and done something to her records. She thought that this was impossible. No one she knew would be so mean to her, she said, and also her house, that day as always, had been securely locked while she had been away.

So exactly what happened to Ruth Ann Bennett's Elvis Presley record collection in August, 1977, remains a mystery. Her case bears a curious similarity, however, to events which were unfolding that day, several hundred miles away.

On a picturesque side street, not too far from the downtown area of a moderate-sized midwestern city, stands a stately, turn-of-the-century house which is a veritable museum of Elvis Presley artifacts. It is the home of Arthur and Marian Parker, an interesting couple who were, respectively, sixty-seven and sixty-five years of age when I visited them in 1979.

They had been married since he was twenty-two and she was twenty. They bought a hardware store when they were quite young and had made their living from the business. Although they both wanted children, they never had any. When Elvis came along in 1956, they instantly became fans, and it is clear that they adopted him as the son they never had. Their collection of Elvis Presley records, pictures, books, posters and movies is immense and spreads over every room in their house. To me, the most spectacular and intriguing item in their collection is a large (four feet by three feet) watercolor painting which hangs in their bedroom, from the wall beside their ornate, antique brass bed. This painting, which was painted by Marian herself and lovingly framed by Arthur, shows Elvis being welcomed into heaven by Jesus. Jesus has his arms opened wide in a greeting, and Elvis, costumed in a gorgeous robe, is reaching out toward Him. To the right of Jesus, and slightly behind him, stands Gladys Presley, Elvis's mother, with a beatific expression on her face. She appears to be moving toward her son as he enters the hereafter. Beautiful, luminescent outlines of heavenly scenery are in the background of the painting, seen as if through a light mist. Marian completed the painting six weeks after Elvis died. She said the inspiration for it came in a dream she had two days after Elvis's funeral.

Neither Arthur nor Marian has any interest in occult or paranormal phenomena. That makes what happened to them on the evening Elvis died seem all the more remarkable. Arthur explained:

66On August 16, 1977, at 5:30 P.M., I drove up in front of our house and parked on the street. As I walked up the sidewalk, leading to the front porch of the house, I glanced at the mailbox to see if there was any mail there, and as I did, I had the impression that someone had been inside my house. I knew it wasn't Marian, though, because we had been at work together all day, and she was in our other car on her way home. She had stopped at the convenience store for a few things. I was on the porch looking at the door to see if it had been tampered with when I saw Marian's car turn the corner down the street. She got out of the car and walked up the sidewalk onto the porch, and when she walked up to me I said, "I have a funny feeling someone has been inside the house."

She looked surprised but she didn't say anything. We looked very carefully at the door but it had not been tampered with, and the lock is a dead bolt. Marian unlocked the door and we went inside. Right away we both noticed that the statue of Elvis which stands on the coffee table in front of the sofa had fallen to the floor and broken. Then we saw that our two favorite pictures of Elvis had fallen from the mantle over the fireplace and the glass in the frames had shattered and was on the floor. One of the pictures was of Elvis with his mother in Graceland, and the other one was of him in his Army uniform. He had autographed the one of him in the Army for us.

Well, the statue and the pictures had fallen. There was no sign that anyone had come into the house. All the windows and doors had been locked and hadn't been bothered. There was no way it could have been a breeze that knocked them down because all the windows had been closed tightly. You asked on the telephone yesterday whether we had a dog or a cat that might have knocked them down, but we haven't had a pet for fifteen years.

We walked around the house and yard for a little while, checking to see if anything else except the pictures and statue had been damaged. Marian asked me if we should call the police, but I didn't know what we would tell them except that the things had fallen. Nothing was missing.

None of our things had ever fallen before. The statue is always placed very carefully in the center of the table and the pictures all the way back on the mantle. We talked for a while about what might have happened. By then it was six o'clock. I turned on the television set to get the news, and the first thing we heard was that Elvis had died. Marian turned white and said, "No, no, no!" and started crying. I was too shocked to say anything. The TV announcers told about how they didn't really know yet what he had died of. They thought it might have been a heart attack. We were both so upset. Naturally we couldn't eat dinner. We couldn't talk about anything but Elvis. We took out our box of pictures of him and looked through them. Then we listened to a special program about him on the radio. For a while we kept watching the television set for bulletins.

You must understand that for us, this was like losing our son. We were always so fond of him. We decided we would go to Memphis the next day. I called the young man who helped us manage our business. Marian was too grief-stricken to talk to him. I told him that we were going to Memphis for a few days and he and our other employee would have to hold down the fort until we got back. It didn't matter that much because we were almost in semi-retirement by that time anyway.

We finally got in bed a little after midnight, after the late news and reports. We were going to try to get some sleep before starting our trip. We stayed awake and talked for a time and then we heard a thump followed by a tremendous crash in the living room. We got out of bed and I turned on the light. When we went into the living room, Marian flipped the light switch and we saw that the statue [they had glued it back together] on the coffee table had fallen off again, and this time an entire wall shelf about three feet long that we keep Elvis souvenirs on had fallen from the wall to the floor [a distance of about five feet] and some of the things on it had broken.

There wasn't anyone around, and definitely Marian and I were in bed talking when it happened. We just didn't understand it. We wondered if someone was playing a trick on us, but it didn't make sense that anybody could be that clever to keep us from seeing him or could be that mean to play such a dirty trick on us, especially knowing that we were both sick. My wife was crying that whole night. She was scared to death and so was I. **"**

Marian corroborated Arthur's account of the events of that evening, and in her retelling emphasized the sense of bafflement that they shared.

"Dr. Moody, if you or any other doctor or scientific person could tell us what in the world happened that night, I would be most indebted to you. You see, we have both worked all our lives and never had any education in college. There must be somebody somewhere who knows about these things, but I sure don't. We didn't talk about it with anybody at work. We didn't know who to talk about it with, so we didn't talk about it with anybody. We heard you lecture at the college and we said, "Well, if anybody knows anything about it, he might." So we decided to ask you about it.

Of course, Arthur and I talked about how it might have been our boy coming to say "good-bye", but I don't think so. I don't think he would come to say "good-bye" in a way that scared us half to death. He was too good a person for that.

While the thing was going on I was scared myself but I was much more worried about Arthur's heart. He had a heart attack already about one year before Elvis died, and I was so worried when we went in the living room and saw the shelf had fallen down. I was worried that Arthur was going to have a heart attack right there and die. **99**

Arthur, too, talked of the feelings of confusion and helplessness the couple had experienced that night.

66I wanted to turn to someone, but who do you turn to for a thing like that? Marian wanted to call the police when the shelf fell, but I said, "Call the police and tell them that a shelf fell?" I was sure that they would ask us if we had been drinking, and neither one of us has ever had more than a few sips of wine in our lives.

So who do you call when something like this happens? You can't call the doctor, because we weren't sick. You can't call the doctor in the middle of the night and say, "I'm calling because a shelf fell." I'm sure our minister would have been nice to us, but he would've thought we were not in our right minds, too. **99**

Finally, Arthur expressed his own opinion concerning the cause of the events of that night. He is strongly convinced that they cannot be explained in terms of any normal phenomena. However, he also doubts that the movements of the objects were caused by the departed spirit of Elvis Presley.

❝Well, I don't know, but I don't put much stock in stories about spirits and the like. I don't believe the spirits of the dead can come back to torment the living. It's against what I am taught in my religion to believe that. Besides, why would Elvis be so noisy when he came back and turn over things? He wasn't like that in life. If he wanted to tell us something, I think he would have chosen a gentler way.❞

Nonetheless, both Marian and Arthur expressed to me their complete certainty that their relationship with Elvis is not over and that they will be with him again — forever — in the life hereafter. As Arthur explains it,

❝I know we'll be with him again someday in eternity. We'll be with our boy in heaven. The Lord Jesus Himself guarantees that to us, that all who love the Lord will be together in heaven. That I know. We'll be together with Elvis again.❞

Before I left Marian and Arthur I told them that, regrettably, I could do little to justify the hope and confidence they had placed in my ability to help them understand their experience. However, I was able to tell them that there is a little-known anomalous psychological phenomenon, studied by only a few professionals, which bears a strong resemblance to the happenings that took place in their home that night. This phenomenon, called poltergeist, is usually confined to a house and consists of strange, loud noises and knockings and inexplicable movements of objects in the household. In the typical case, ceramic vases, pictures hung from walls, bric-a-brac, and sometimes heavy items of furniture will fly off shelves or overturn. The movements appear to bystanders to have an almost magical quality. Although no simple explanation for these happenings is universally accepted, there are clearly patterns to the activity. Almost invariably, a young person — most often a child around the age of puberty — will seem to be the "focus" of the disturbances. That is, the movements take place only or almost always when the child is present in the house. However, instances of movements have been observed by reliable investigators in situations in which the child involved could not possibly have moved the object by any known physical means. Poltergeist activity usually lasts only for a short period of time — a few days or weeks — and then ceases. These occurrences have been reported for centuries; John Wesley, one of the founders of the Methodist faith, was involved directly in one case.

I reported on the events experienced by the Parkers to a professor of psychology who is a renowned expert on poltergeist phenomena, having investigated many cases in his long career. He assures me that the disturbances at the Parker household can be characterized as a poltergeist. It differs in some way from the typical case, however, in that no young person who seemed to be the "focus" of the movements lived in or was present in the house at the time. In summary, the events which the Parkers related to me, baffling as they seem, do have precedents. What they mean is, I presume, anyone's guess.

Janice McMichael never imagined, when Elvis Presley gave her his jacket in 1975, that it would ever be anything more than a treasured keepsake. Now, it seems, the jacket has almost taken on a life of its own, and sometimes she wonders whether she should even keep it around. I spoke with Janice in a restaurant in Washington, D.C., during the summer of 1986. She was thirty-nine; an attractive brunette, she was then working as a secretary in a university. Earlier in her life, she had briefly known Elvis Presley.

“I went around with Elvis in the early seventies. It was nothing serious on his part, though I certainly had my own fantasies. I was trying to get work in the entertainment business during that period. I am a pretty good actress, but I found out fast that it is hard to get into show business no matter what your talents. I am from Ohio and I left home when I was twenty-one to go scouting for acting jobs in California. I am one of the lucky ones because I actually did get parts on a couple of shows. Never enough to make a living at it, though.

A mutual friend introduced me to Elvis in the early 1970's. Elvis Presley was a really nice guy. When he gave a party, he wasn't satisfied until he saw every person and asked them where they were from and a little bit about them. He was sweet. I don't know how else to put it. I don't know exactly how many times I saw him. Five or six times maybe. I never saw him on any regular schedule. I would love to be able to tell you I was a special lover of Elvis Presley but I wasn't, really.

At the time I knew him, Elvis was quite concerned about death. He didn't look well. But that tender personality beamed right through. We talked about death a good deal. He wanted to know what I thought about death. I remember thinking, "Here is a man with all the money in the world and he wants something money cannot buy him. He wants to know about death." That was one of my interests, too, so we talked. The last time I saw him was a couple of years before he died. I can't tell you for sure what year it was. I think 1975. I was leaving the place where we were. It was cold and rainy. I wasn't dressed heavily because I had arrived on the plane from Southern California where it was warm. Elvis gave me a light tan jacket he had. I had noticed that giving people things seemed sort of automatic to him. He never seemed to think anything about it.

I think before I got to know Elvis, I was awed. Once I got to know him, I saw something of the vulnerability. He had a way of putting people at ease. He was easy to talk to. Although I was not particularly awed by Elvis, the jacket was a special present to me. It reminded me of the old saying about the friend who would give you the shirt off his back. I bought a plastic hanging bag for the jacket and I keep it in my closet. I have moved three times since I got it, and it always goes in the car with me to the new apartment.

Elvis's death hit me like a ton of bricks. I didn't find out about it until the day after it happened. I stayed home all that day writing letters and listening to tapes. It wasn't until the next morning when my clock radio alarm went off that I heard about it. I woke up to the news that Elvis Presley had died the day before. It's odd, but two or three days before I had a passing thought that I should get in touch with Elvis. I knew his health wasn't good. It crossed my mind that he wasn't going to live forever and I should see him again. It's odd that I would think of him dying only two days before he did die.

Elvis's death rattled me personally. I became very anxious. Sometimes my hands would shake. I worried about my health and death all the time for maybe six months. Elvis had seemed immortal. He was the first person I had ever known to die. Even my two grandmothers were alive then. I had never known my grandfathers. They died before I was born. So Elvis happened to be the first person I knew well who died. So for six months I was scared to death of death.

It didn't help much that the jacket Elvis gave me started acting up around that time. Twice within a week the jacket fell to the floor of the closet while I was at work. Never in all the time I had it did it fall, and then it fell twice in a week. I can't tell you for sure how long after Elvis died it was that the jacket fell. About a month probably. Surely no longer than two months. The first time I found it on the closet floor I had an eerie feeling. I'll be honest and tell you, yes, I did wonder when I saw the jacket on the floor if Elvis had been trying to get my attention from the other side. After the second time it fell, I took it out of the hang-up bag and left it hanging in the closet.

I do remember that it was in November that the jacket really got active. It fell off the hanger three times in early November, once when I was looking straight at it. Oh, I would say I was about five feet away, I guess. I saw it fall that time, definitely. This was in the broad daylight, too. I couldn't imagine why the jacket would fall like that. This was eerie.

Not many people know where that jacket came from. My mother is one, a couple of others, including my sister. I know what would happen if anyone knew where the jacket came from. I would have a burglary, I'm sure. I know a man who mentioned in a bar one day that he had a collection of Elvis records with the original Sun label. Less than a week later, someone broke into his house and stole all his records. You can't let people know you have Elvis Presley momentos around. Not if you want to keep them.

Elvis had left a couple of facial tissues in the right pocket of the jacket when he gave it to me. And there was a penny in there. I got a laugh out of that one — a penny in the pocket of a multi-millionaire's jacket! The kleenex and the penny are still in the pocket. I wouldn't ever separate them.

I got so nervous after Elvis died that I took in a room-mate. Her name was Mary and she was from Oklahoma. She came here to work for the government. I was afraid of someone trying to get in the apartment and finding me alone, so I let Mary live there with me and share the rent. That's the only time I ever felt nervous about being alone, for about six months after Elvis died.

Mary moved in in January. The November before was when the jacket got so active and fell three times. Then on November 20th, 1977, I woke up in the middle of the night. There is a nightlight in the hall outside my bed-room and the light shines almost directly in on the closet. The closet is the kind with two sliding doors, and one of the doors was all the way back. So the closet was open on the side the jacket is in. I don't know why I woke up. I looked over at the closet. I kept trying to focus my eyes because I couldn't believe what I was seeing. The jacket sleeve was moving, bending all the way up and then back down. It would've been the right sleeve of the jacket. I know because that is the way the jacket was hanging in the closet. I was petrified. I tried to move but couldn't. It was like I was paralyzed. I can't tell you how long this went on. Maybe ten minutes, maybe thirty. Once in a while the sleeve of the jacket would move up slowly and then down again. I was unable to move, and then finally I went back to sleep. When I woke up in the morning, the jacket was on the hanger. It hadn't fallen. I never saw the jacket moving around like that again.

As I said, Mary moved in in January. She had a dog, Sparky, a miniature collie. Sometimes that dog would go up to my closet and bark. She would always be near the jacket when she barked. Then after a few weeks, she wouldn't go near the closet at all. She would act scared when she was near it. Mary said, "Janice, what do you have in the closet? Sparky thinks there is something in there."

I never told Mary about the jacket or how I got it. In February a woman moved into the apartment down the hall. I got to know her well. Her name was Alice. She was interested in psychics and all that. As a matter of fact, she took me to a conference on psychics here in Washington. One day when I was having tea in her apartment, I brought up that I had had some odd experiences with a jacket in my closet. I told her an old friend gave it to me. I didn't tell her who. She went into my apartment and looked around. She told me she would get a "reading" on the jacket. She told me the jacket belonged to a highly spiritual man who died young. I was amazed and told her that was right. She said she heard beautiful music around the jacket. I didn't hear any music, that's for sure, but she was right about the owner dying young.

Only one other weird thing happened with the jacket after that. In late February, I was sliding the jacket over to the side of the rack to put some of my clothes in there. When I touched the jacket at the top, I noticed it was wet. It was damp all around the collar, which is knit. There was no reason for that jacket to get wet. That got me upset again. Mary didn't like Washington and moved away the first of March. I was alone again, still worried about dying, still kind of scared about the jacket.

On March 21st, I had a dream. Elvis and I were walking through the woods. It was a gorgeous place out in the country. We were surrounded by huge, green mountains. The sky was an incredibly deep blue. I could see birds of every color of the rainbow flying around. We walked along a path. There were brightly colored flowers blooming all around us. Elvis held my hand as we walked along. This dream was so real. The moment I woke up I wrote it all down. We walked over a brook on a stone bridge. Elvis talked with me. I wrote down exactly what he said when I woke up. We sat down on the stone bridge. He held my hand and hugged me close. He said, "Janice, you are kinda slow, aren't you? Don't you remember how we used to talk about death? We wanted to know whether we would live after we die. I've been trying to get through to you through the jacket, honey, but you're getting scared. It didn't work. I want to let you know that we do live after we die. So go on and live."

He held me very close and said good-bye. Then he smiled that sweet smile of his and he took the jacket he was wearing in the dream off and put it on me. This jacket was made out of some material like silk. It was yellow. Very pretty. That was the end of the dream. I woke up and immediately wrote the whole dream down.

Since March 21st, 1978, I haven't given death a second thought. The dream made me feel better instantly. The jacket is still in my closet. I'm not scared of it anymore. I'll keep it always. Elvis Presley will be in my heart always. **99**

Because I was in Washington for only two days to attend a professional conference, I didn't have time to go to Janice's apartment to see the jacket for myself. I thanked her for sharing her intensely personal experience with me. When she asked whether I had ever heard of anything like this before, I outlined the two other experiences involving unusual effects on objects that I've already reported in this chapter. I also told her that the experience she had of lying in bed unable to move and seeing the jacket move reminded me of a little-known medical condition called sleep paralysis. This phenomenon is rare, and the people to whom it happens seem more susceptible to it during periods in which they are anxious or under stress, as Janice was at the time. Victims of sleep paralysis wake up from sleep feeling fully alert, awake and aware but unable to move even a muscle and feeling quite scared and anxious. Sometimes the state is associated with what is called hypnopompic imagery, vivid images that appear, for all the world, real. Perhaps what had happened to her on that night, I suggested, had been an episode of sleep paralysis with vivid imagery of the jacket moving — in effect, a waking dream. I had no explanations for the jacket's falling, however, and I commented that obviously the dream had brought about a resolution of the mourning process for Elvis that she was going through at the time.

Janice is an articulate, stable, and intelligent young woman. Her experience has no doubt left her a changed and happier person. She owes a lot, she contends, to her friendship with Elvis Presley.

CHAPTER VI

In Search Of A Son With Elvis

HAROLD WELCH HAS BEEN A policeman in a small Georgia city for over fifteen years. He is a large, tough-looking man who says that he is proud to be the son of a textile mill worker. He is surprisingly gentle and soft-spoken in manner, but it is still hard to picture him as having had an uncanny psychic experience, much less speaking so straightforwardly about it. As he recounted his intriguing story, I had the distinct impression that he was describing events just as he remembered them, with no embellishment and with minimal interpretation. He spoke with me in a small, windowless conference room in a plain, one-story brick building which serves as both the city hall and police station of the town in which he lives.

66This happened in 1982, in the month of March, to be exact. I was having a lot of trouble with my youngest son, Tony, then. He got in with a rough crowd and they were caught shoplifting downtown. His mother and I knew that he was smoking marijuana around that time because it got back to us by the grapevine. I never could catch him with it. I always swore to all my sons that if I caught them with drugs I would turn them in just as I would any other offender, and I would see to it that the judge would be as hard on them as with anyone else.

Tony was the only one of my sons that ever got into any trouble. He is a good boy but fell in with the wrong group. Sometimes he would be out until all hours marauding. We sort of lost control of him for a while. There was a big confrontation with him in the early part of February, 1982. He was a junior in high school at that time and his grades had gone way down below his capabilities. My wife had surgery on her back that year and was in the hospital for a month, then was laid up at home for quite a while after that. Once or twice a week there would be what you would call a loud discussion with tears about his grades, his drinking and the company he kept. On February 3rd or 4th of that year he came home about three A.M., drunk. My wife and I had been worried about him and I had been out for two hours in my car looking all over town for him. When he finally came in, I blew my top. I said some things I shouldn't have. Any father will know what I mean.

He didn't say a word to us for the next three or four days. When he was home, he would be in his room playing his records. Tony liked Elvis Presley and country singers. He never liked the weird rock 'n' roll groups most of the teenagers get into these days. Always Elvis. His room was full of Elvis posters. I liked it that he had this feeling for Elvis. It was better by a long shot than listening to some of those crazy bands that you read about being heavy into drugs.

Tony knew everything there was to know about Elvis Presley. I didn't have any real strong reaction to Elvis either way. The closest I ever came to him was when I was called in for extra security when he put on a show in a city near here. I didn't get anywhere near Elvis. I never even saw him.

Tony had this idea that he would go off to California and get into the movies. He had saved up quite a bit of money, over two thousand dollars, I think. A week after that blowup, he took off without a word to us. He was gone.

I have been in law enforcement for almost twenty years, and I know there is not much parents can do under these circumstances. My wife almost went off the deep end. She cried for two weeks straight. I took to chain smoking. I had been a smoker since I was twelve years old, but I was off them then because of severe bronchitis and trouble getting my breath. While Tony was gone, I was back to three packs a day.

I felt sure he had gone to California. I also knew that children out there don't have a snowball's chance in a blast furnace. I knew if he was out there long he would be out of money and would turn to dope pushing or worse. My son Harold, Jr., the oldest of the four boys, works for the Atlanta police department and has had experience with missing children. So the two of us took a notion to go out to Los Angeles and try to track Tony down.

Tony left on February 11th and Harold, Jr., and I were to leave to fly out there on March 3rd. The doctor had my wife on sleeping pills at that time. She couldn't sleep from worrying about Tony. Every time the phone rang she would get upset. So finally I moved out of our bedroom into the living room. I took the phone with me into the living room so she would sleep. I slept on the sofa at night and I would answer all phone calls. Most of them at night were for the other son who lived at home. I guess I was expecting every phone call to be from Tony.

On the night of March 1st I was sleeping on the sofa in the living room and I had a dream about Elvis Presley. In the dream Elvis walked into my office. He told me he had some information about Tony for me. As near as I can remember, he said, "I'm worried about Tony, sir. Tony is a fan of mine. He's out there in Los Angeles and I can't get through to him." Elvis was wearing regular street clothes except that he had on a light police jacket. He showed me a badge. I have a map of the city on the wall behind my desk, but in the dream Elvis pointed to the map and I saw that it was a map of Los Angeles instead. He tried to show me some streets in a certain area of Los Angeles, but I had never been out there so I couldn't focus on the map. I couldn't make out any street names, as hard as I tried.

Elvis gave up then. He started talking to me. He said, "Look, Tony is staying in a rooming house." Then I saw, or Elvis showed me, a scene. There was a short street with a drugstore on the corner and a short-order diner across from it. Suddenly, Elvis and I were right there on that street, walking down it. Everything seemed blurred. I couldn't see too well. Elvis kept trying to point out things to me so I would recognize them. Elvis grabbed me by the arm and shook me. He said, "Look, man, you gotta look at this. This is important, man." He showed me an old house. It was run-down. Seedy looking. Elvis said, "Man, your son is on drugs. You gotta get him some help." I could tell he was trying to get me to look at that old house. It was a two-story house. I saw a cat on the front steps trying to get in the door. It looked like it belonged there. It was an orange colored cat with stripes.

Elvis was trying real hard to get across the name of the street to me, but I never could make it out. Elvis looked just like he did in his pictures. In the dream he was about six-feet tall and he looked to be thirty years old. I got a good look at him but the surroundings were blurred. I kept trying to focus on the house but I could only see it through a blur. Elvis was trying to help me. I thanked him. He impressed me as a concerned man.

I woke up from the dream with a headache and this ringing in my ears. Now, you may think I'm nuts, but I woke up knowing that I would find Tony. All that next day I dwelled on that dream. It impressed me that Elvis had a badge. I knew about his support of law enforcement. I had not ever dreamed about Elvis Presley before. The dream seemed completely real.

Harold, Jr., and I flew to Los Angeles on March 3rd. We went right to work. I made some contacts with law enforcement officers out there. They were cooperative. We talked with a man who is an expert on this kind of work. He directed us to some areas of town where a lot of kids hang out. We passed out pictures of Tony. We got some leads from a lot of people in the area, but no one remembered seeing Tony.

Harold, Jr., rented a car. We drove all through those areas the expert had designated. On March 9th I was driving. I saw a drugstore and the short-order hamburger stand across from it that was in the dream. Now, you're saying, "This man has lost his mind." But, nope, Dr.

Moody, this happened to me. I saw that drugstore and I saw that short-order place, and I said to myself, "This is the street Elvis Presley showed me in the dream." It was two o'clock in the afternoon.

I turned to Harold, Jr., who was in the front seat on the passenger's side. I said, "Son, this is where we'll find Tony." I think Harold, Jr., thought his old man had flipped his lid. Anyway, I had pulled over to the curb and stopped in front of the drugstore. I turned to the right down that street, and about half a block down the street I saw three old two-story houses. The whole street seemed familiar to me. Now, I don't know how to tell you this, but I knew that was the street I walked down with Elvis in that dream.

I couldn't tell at first which one of the three houses it was that Elvis showed me in the dream. The only part of the house I saw real clearly in the dream was the front door and the front steps. So I looked closely at the doors, and the front door and steps of one of the houses looked like the one in the dream. I went up to that house and knocked on the door. An old woman with a cane came and opened it. I noticed that the front door had glass on the top half and there were thin white curtains on the inside covering the glass. Almost like gauze. They were just slightly parted. I had seen those same curtains in the dream.

My heart was almost pounding out of my chest when she opened the door. She looked at me. She seemed almost alarmed. I think she thought I was crazy or something. She said, "What is it? Can I help you?" I said, "Ma'am, do you have a Tony Welch living here?" She said, "Well, yes, I do."

I told her I was his father and he was missing from home. I said I had to see him right away. She motioned upstairs and pointed to his room opening onto the landing. Now, at this point Harold, Jr., was in a fog. I hadn't told him about the dream. He looked confused, but he followed me upstairs.

When I got to Tony's room, I knocked on the door. I heard him say, "Come in." I opened that door and took one step in. The boy was sprawled out on the bed reading a magazine. I looked right into his face and grinned. He turned white as a sheet. He said, "Dad, how did you find me?" He burst out crying and jumped up and came over to me.

I stood there hugging that boy for a minute. I cried, too. He said, "Dad, I want to go back home."

We packed up all his things. I paid the landlady off. As we were getting ready to walk out the door I asked her, "Ma'am, do you have a cat?" She said, "Well, no I don't." I asked her if there was an orange striped cat living anywhere around the neighborhood. I wanted to know about that cat I saw in the dream. I was so sure it lived around there. She said no, she didn't know of any cat like that. She didn't ask me why I wanted to know. From the way I was acting and from the way Harold, Jr., looked, I guess she figured by then that we belonged in the loony bin.

On the way back to the hotel in the car, Harold, Jr., and Tony kept asking me how I knew. I never did tell them. To tell you the truth, I would have been too embarrassed to tell my sons Elvis showed me the street in a dream. I kept it to myself. Harold, Jr., thinks that I found out from one of the policemen in the L.A. Police Department and that for some reason I didn't want to divulge my source. I didn't tell him that. That's something he came up with.

That night in the hotel room, Tony and I chewed the fat a long time. He said, "Dad, it's the funniest thing. Two times since I've been out here I've had dreams about Elvis Presley. In both dreams he told me you would be coming to get me. He said he was worried about me. He said he would work it out."

I started crying when I heard that, but I still couldn't bring myself to tell the boy about the dream. I still haven't told him, but I've gotten up the nerve. I'm going to tell him soon.

It was true what Elvis said in the dream about the drugs. Tony was on drugs. We got him help and he is over that now. He is doing well. All straightened out.

I don't know what to make of that dream. Nothing like that ever happened to me before or since. I am a no-nonsense person. I have to be in my line of work. I have never had any involvement with these psychic things. A few years back in a city near here there was a big murder case that was causing a big row. It was all over the papers. They brought in these psychics, if that's what you call them, to help. I thought it was bunk, myself.

Now I don't know what to think. It seems to me that Elvis Presley was worried about my son and came in a dream to help. I don't know what else to think.**

Harold Welch's story is one of the most baffling I have encountered. If the facts are as he remembered and reported them, the story defies simple explanation. Harold seemed to be to be a reliable, sincere and rational person, not prone to fantasizing.

The dream itself, no doubt, suggests some interesting psychological dynamics. In a way, Harold was *identifying* with Elvis in the dream. Elvis appeared as a figure who was concerned about Tony, as Harold obviously was at the time of the dream, and as a police officer, which is Harold's occupation. The difficulty Elvis alluded to in the dream of "getting through" to Tony echoes the trouble Harold was having in communicating with his son.

The uncanny "confirmation" of the places portrayed in the dream, however, seems to give the dream a reality of some kind independent of Harold's mind. Like Harold himself, I hardly know what to think.

CHAPTER VII

An American Trilogy

THREE OF THE CASES I have gathered in the course of doing the research for this volume don't seem to fit any particular pattern. Each is unique in its own right; each speaks for itself. They happened, at various times and in widely separated regions of the country, to very different kinds of people.

Polly Tyson, when I visited her in her quaint Victorian home in a little Massachusetts town in August of 1979, struck me as a down-to-earth, likable soul, the kind of person neighbors always feel comfortable in asking for help or advice when problems arise. Within a couple of hours after I arrived to find her sitting on her spacious front porch, swaying gently back and forth in her creaky antique porch swing, savoring a nice late afternoon breeze, I came to realize that her kitchen was the social hub for the women in her neighborhood.

Polly at that time was forty-two, though — as she herself brought to my attention — she looked somewhat
older. Her intense blue eyes looked out with compassion
from under a shock of reddish-orange hair, and her figure was as wiry as the thin metal frames of her glasses.
There were wrinkles in her face, it is true, but they were
not at all unpleasing to the eye. Clearly, they were somehow an engraved record of the troubles she had had in
her life: Her first husband had died when she was only
twenty-five, leaving her two young sons to raise alone.
She had remarried at age thirty-six, only to find out
within a few weeks that her second husband was an alcoholic. She had divorced him three years later. Through it
all, Polly was optimistic and enjoyed a successful career
as an office manager for a large appliance store.

Her love for Elvis Presley had been a constant fixture
in Polly's life since she was nineteen years old. She still
had the original 45-rpm records of his songs which she
had purchased as a teen-ager, and it was plain that she
knew a great deal about him. She showed me her three
enormous, thick scrapbooks of pictures, clippings, photographs and newspaper and magazine articles on Elvis,
dating back to 1956, the year she had first begun to idol-
ize him. Like so many in her age range, she took Elvis as
a symbol of much that was important during the fifties,
sixties and seventies: to her, he was still and would forever remain "The King."

I already knew the outline of the story she was to tell
me on that warm, late-summer day. She had written it to
me in a letter a few weeks before. Now I had come to
meet her personally and to see for myself the mysterious
phenomenon she had written about in her letter. One
year and seven months before, quite suddenly and mirac-

ulously in her view, an image of Elvis had appeared on her pantry door. I wanted to make sure that I had recorded Polly's recollection of the event thoroughly before I gazed on the baffling image. I switched on my tape recorder.

66The first year after Elvis died was real hard for me, Dr. Moody. I remember exactly where I was when I heard about it. We were having a bake sale for our church and I was at our booth at the shopping center. I had baked three cakes and a man had just bought one of them. Two women walked by. One of them had on a pink dress that looked a little too small for her, and the other woman was younger and was wearing a yellow skirt with a white blouse. I thought she must have been the older woman's daughter. The younger woman was carrying her son, a little boy around two years old, and he looked like he was almost asleep. The older woman had tears in her eyes, and her daughter was trying to comfort her. I heard her saying, "Don't worry, Momma. I'll drive you home. I don't think you should be out shopping today if you are so upset."

The older woman looked so sad I could tell something terrible had happened to her. Her daughter looked like she felt sorry for her mother but didn't know what to do. So I said, "Is there anything I can do to help you?"

And the younger woman said, "No, she'll be all right. She just found out that Elvis Presley has died."

It hit me like a rifle shot. I didn't believe it at first, but when it finally registered I was speechless. The first thought I remember having was, "Oh, no. He's dead and I never did get to meet him." To meet Elvis always had been a cherished dream of mine, and now I knew it was never to be. I felt a sinking in the pit of my stomach. Then I started crying, too. The tears flowed out of my eyes like water out of a leaky bucket.

Without a moment's thought I stood up and walked out onto the sidewalk from behind the booth, and I grabbed onto the older woman and we stood there hugging and crying together for what seemed like five minutes. And this was a woman I had never seen before in my life. I still run into her once in a while downtown and we talk about that day.

Two weeks after Elvis died, I came down with a bad stomach infection. It lasted almost two weeks. My doctor told me I was having a virus, but, myself, I know that I got sick because I was grieving so over Elvis. For a whole year after he died, I was in and out of the sickbed, which is unusual for me. I'm hardly ever sick.

Doris Taylor, my best friend, came over a lot that year. We would sit in the kitchen at my old round oak table and drink coffee and talk. Sometimes we would talk and cry about Elvis. Myself, I think that if a picture of Elvis had been on the pantry door we would have seen it long before that day. We had always sat right there at the table in the same places. I think we would've seen it, if it had been there.

The day we saw it happened oddly enough to be a few days after Elvis's birthday. It was a sad day because it was his first birthday after he died. This is corny, I know, Dr. Moody, but it is something only a dyed-in-the-wool Elvis fan would understand: On his birthday that year, Doris and I had a birthday celebration for him. We had banana splits, which he liked, and Dreamsicles, and we played

Elvis records for a long time. That may sound corny, but I bet a lot of his other fans did things like that, too.

Anyway, it wasn't more than three or four days after that that we saw the image. Doris was sitting across from me, where she always sat. There is a pantry in the kitchen with a thick, solid walnut door. This house was built in the 1870's, I'm told, and as far as I know, that door has been here ever since the house was built. The pantry door, as you will see when we go in there, is dark wood, and solid and thick.

That day I was sitting with my back to the pantry door and Doris was sitting across from me at the table, so she had a straight view at the door. We hadn't been talking for a few seconds, just sipping coffee. I looked across the table at Doris, and she looked white as a ghost. She was staring at the door.

She said, "Polly, I see Elvis's face on your pantry door."

When she said that, I didn't know what she was talking about. The first thing that popped into my mind, before I turned around to look, was that my son Travis must have drawn a picture of Elvis on the door. Travis is always playing tricks on me and has always kidded me about Elvis. But then I thought Travis wouldn't do such a thing as draw on my door. Besides, by the time I had turned around and saw what Doris was talking about, I knew that neither Travis nor anyone else could have drawn something like that.

Doris had to show me part of the outline of the face before I saw it. But as soon as she pointed and said, "See, here's his hair," I saw the whole face, all the way down to his mid-chest level, just as plain as day. It was Elvis, all right, no mistake about it. There was Elvis Presley's face looking right out at us from my pantry door.

We talked about it for a long time that night. Doris called her mother-in-law, who lives down the street and who likes Elvis, to come see it, and we showed it to a few of the other women in the neighborhood, but mostly I have kept quiet about it. I wouldn't want to create a ruckus and have people tramping through here night and day to see it. I wouldn't want to have that as a routine thing, no, sir. Doris wanted to call a friend of her husband's who works at the paper and let them do a story on it, but I said, "No way!" **"**

Polly led me out of her elegantly furnished living room, down a hall and into her cozy kitchen. Then she directed my attention toward the dark, wooden door.

I can't deny it. Immediately I saw the likeness of Elvis Presley, unmistakably, there in the door. Frankly, I had expected that the image would be very difficult to see, that I would have to do a great deal of squinting and exercise my imagination terrifically, before I would be able to see what they were talking about. Instead, the image was plain, almost stark.

I looked at it from several angles and several distances. I found that I could see the image most plainly when I was standing about four or five feet away from and directly in front of the door. Although the features of Elvis are formed out of patterns in the natural grain of the wood, the image itself seemed almost to float a min-ute distance in front of the surface of the wood, almost as though one could see the door *through* the image.

I stood there for quite some time while Polly chatted amiably. "Doris's husband, Herbert, told her that he bets somebody just painted it on there, but that makes me mad, because he has never even been over here to see it. Nobody could have painted that, Dr. Moody."

Polly didn't even have to say that; it was obvious that the image of Elvis came from the patterns and lines and swirls in the grain of the wood. No artist, no matter how skilled, could have painted the image I saw embedded deeply within the very wood itself.

As I sat there in her kitchen, comfortable and relaxed, I knew what the "natural," "rational" explanation would be. The "image" simply resulted, so such an explanation would go, from the combination of lines and patterns in the wood which had been there all along. Doris assembled the lines into an image of Elvis on that day simply because she had been thinking of him. Calling the pattern of lines a picture of Elvis focused the attention of others on it, too, and they could see the pattern as a likeness of Elvis as well. On this level, it is no different from the well-known phenomenon of seeing faces and animals and scenes in billowing white clouds against blue skies on bright summer days. Not only can we see things in clouds, we can point them out to others and help them to see the same patterns we see.

This much, I suppose, is a given about Polly's experience. The psychological and, perhaps, even spiritual truth of the matter, however, is deeper and more poignant than that. To Polly, what happened to her on that day is imbued with a meaning which has helped her surmount her grief over the personal loss she felt at the death of Elvis Presley. She smiled as she explained it to me.

“Every morning when I am in my kitchen making breakfast, and every evening when I am in there cooking supper, I am cheerful. Before this happened, and after Elvis died, I had been feeling sad and miserable. I was feeling sorry for myself, I guess. Not any more. Now I know life goes on. The birds still sing every day in the spring and summer outside my window. And I feel like Elvis is there with me, right there in the kitchen, looking out at me from the door. And it makes me happy. Of course, I really know that it isn't the image on the door that counts. What counts is that he is there with me in my heart. And there, he'll always be. **"**

In the winter of 1985, when I visited them in their snug little house in the Oregon countryside, Nancy Morgan was thirty-three and her son, Jeremy, was six and a half years old. Two weeks earlier, Nancy had telephoned me to say that she had learned of my interest in unusual experiences involving Elvis from an acquaintance of hers. Although she was reluctant to discuss what was going on with her and Jeremy over the phone, she thought it would fit in with my study and in any event she wanted to talk with me about it in person. She invited me to come visit them, and I accepted.

When I arrived, Nancy and Jeremy greeted me at the door and led me into their living room. I noticed that there were several pictures of Elvis on the walls. There was a nice wood fire in a cavernous, old-fashioned brick fireplace. Nancy, a slender, attractive blonde, with ethereal blue eyes and a tender smile, told me that she had been divorced from her husband since before Jeremy had been born and that he had become a drifter. She had never seen him or heard from him since the divorce, and she had raised Jeremy alone. She told me that she had been an Elvis fan for as long as she could remember. She had a big collection of his records and had seen all his movies.

Then, getting quickly down to her point in having me there, she announced with obvious sincerity and with complete conviction that Jeremy Morgan was the reincarnation of Elvis Presley. As I sat there on the sofa, wondering how she had arrived at this strange conclusion, she spoke quickly and crisply.

"When Elvis died, I felt as though I had lost my best friend. I had married my husband, Willie, right out of high school, and the main thing I remember, besides Elvis dying, from that whole year of 1977 was fighting with my husband. When Elvis died, I got so depressed I made myself sick. I thought I was going to die.

Willie and I started going to see our minister in October of 1977. We went to see him twice a week and we talked to him about our marriage. By Christmas of that year, we had pretty much made up and a little while after that I found out I was pregnant. When I told Willie about it, he was furious. He yelled at me and said I should have been more careful, like it was all my fault. Anyway, he stayed around a couple of months more and then he left and I haven't seen him since. His cousin told me that he's just drifting around.

I missed Elvis a lot more than I missed my husband. Many nights, while I was pregnant, I would stay up late at night crying about Elvis. I would say, "Elvis, where are you? Why did you die and leave us?" Several nights I would dream about Elvis. One night I dreamed about him and, when I woke up from the dream, I thought for a few moments that Elvis was there in the bedroom with me.

While I was carrying Jeremy, it never occurred to me to think that the baby inside me was Elvis. Once, I thought for a little while of naming the baby after Elvis, if it was a boy, but then, I thought, "No, that would be too much to bear, to have to think of Elvis being dead every time I called my son."

The baby was due on August 12th, but I wondered if it was going to be born on August 16th, which would be exactly one year after Elvis died. August 12th came and no baby, so at one point I was almost sure it would be born on August 16th. But it wasn't. Then on August 18th, I went into labor and my sister and her husband drove me to the hospital and Jeremy was born at 7:30 that night, one year and two days to the day after Elvis died.

It didn't occur to me right after he was born that Jeremy was Elvis. No, not at all. No, it was much later. He was a good baby. Real cute. He slept a lot. He wasn't much trouble at all. He liked to play in his playpen. He would play in there and I would talk to him while I ironed. I would play Elvis Presley records for him a lot and he liked them. He would bounce in time to the music and smile.

I was raised a Baptist in a very fundamental church. My mother talked in tongues and I was baptized in the Holy Spirit when I was fourteen. Reincarnation was never taught in my church and I never believed in it or thought about it.

When I finally realized that Jeremy was Elvis, he was almost eighteen months old. One day I was playing with him and I noticed something about his eyes. They were exactly like Elvis's. I thought, "I wonder if Jeremy could be Elvis Presley come back?" It struck me, and I don't know why. He had always liked Elvis's music. He kind of looked like Elvis in the eyes. I had been thinking of Elvis a lot while I was pregnant and there was that one night I had the impression Elvis was in the room with me while I was pregnant with Jeremy.

So I looked right into Jeremy's eyes and I said, "Jeremy, are you Elvis?" He laughed and I'm sure he knew what I was talking about. He said, "Uh-huh" and nodded his head yes. I was excited and wanted to tell everybody, but I didn't because I knew they would think that I was a nut. The only person I told was my sister. I went to her house with Jeremy that night and when we were together alone in her kitchen, I said, "Ruth, do you think there is anything special about Jeremy?"

She said, "Well, I don't know, but sometimes I have wondered if he might be Elvis Presley reincarnated."

I was really out of breath when she told me that. She had noticed the same things I had. She told me that one night when she and her husband were baby-sitting Jeremy while I went out on a date, he had said, "Elvis like peanut butter and banana." Well, the amazing thing about that was that none of us knew that and it wasn't until months later that we found out that it was true. Elvis really did like peanut butter and banana sandwiches. We read about it months after that night in Ruth's kitchen. So how could Jeremy know something about Elvis that none of us knew?

Ever since that day I have known in my heart that Jeremy is Elvis. I know that Jeremy is going to make a big splash in this life, too. He may not be a singer this time, but he will be very famous and very popular. You may not believe it, but it is true and it will be true for the world to see.

Just about a year ago I went to a psychic. The psychic didn't know a thing about me and I didn't let on a thing. She took me by the hand and she told me a lot of things about myself that nobody knew but me. The last thing she told me was that I had a child and that he was a very special child and that he had been a very famous man in his past life. She said that jillions of people had loved him and that he was going to be famous in this life, too. I didn't tell her but I knew exactly what she was talking about. I didn't tell her that I already knew that Jeremy was Elvis.

So, I am trying hard to provide for Jeremy and to give him what he needs. He is going to be a very important and popular person one day. **"**

When Nancy finished telling me her unusual tale, she got up and walked away into the kitchen. In a short while she returned, bringing with her a big tray with a plate piled high with sandwiches. As the three of us ate, I talked with Jeremy. I wanted to know what his reaction was to Nancy's beliefs. "Jeremy," I asked, "what do you think of what your mother has told me? Do you think you are Elvis?" I admitted to them both that I felt quite strange asking this question of a six-year-old boy.

Jeremy had no hesitation in answering me. "Yeah," he said, "I'm Elvis Presley. I died and I came back."

"How long have you believed this, Jeremy?" I asked. "Do you remember when you first thought about this?"

"I've always known I was Elvis, since I was born," he assured me, not batting an eye. "I came back to be with my mom. She was sad about me and I came to be with her."

There was no mistaking that Jeremy spoke in a voice that sounded something like Elvis's. The inflection, the accent, the intonation — all were similar, even eerily reminiscent of the singer's famous drawl. No doubt, I mused, he had listened to Elvis's voice carefully, under Nancy's tutelage, since he was in the crib.

I asked him what he wanted to become when he grew up. "I don't know yet," he said. "Maybe I'll sing. Maybe I'll be on television. I might be a pilot."

As I talked with Jeremy, it gradually dawned on me that despite his unusual belief about his identity, he seemed to have a healthy emotional adjustment. He was obviously above average in intelligence and he was doing well in school. Neither his friends nor his teachers knew the secret of his identity, he told me when I asked. His mother had instructed him not to tell.

There was little doubt in my mind that Nancy had implanted and encouraged this belief in Jeremy by educating him concerning Elvis Presley's music, personality and life. In effect, I thought, in a home in which there was no father, Nancy had created an "imaginary father" for her son in the form of an elaborate imaginative fantasy. This had the effect of giving Jeremy a male figure on whom to model himself, and he had identified with this figure — Elvis.

As I was preparing to leave, Nancy told me that they wanted to show me one more thing.

"Watch this," Nancy said, talking to me and nodding toward Jeremy, who immediately took his cue. I gazed in amazement as the child began to sing, "Don't Be Cruel," in a close imitation of Elvis's voice, gyrating and gesturing in a near-perfect rendition of the movements and style of his mother's hero.

When the performance was over, I thanked them both for their kindness and hospitality during an unforgettable evening. Then I left, wondering what would become of them.

Although Harry and Vanessa Grant are not sure that their story involves any unusual psychic happenings, it is remarkable enough to warrant inclusion in this volume. For Vanessa and Harry have a unique pastime activity; the two of them frequently wile away the evening hours "talking" with Elvis Presley on their home computer.

The Grants live in a neat and comfortable suburban house outside of Washington, D.C. They are in their late thirties and both say that they have been Elvis fans for as long as they can remember. They met in high school and married soon after they graduated. At that time, Harry started to work with the Postal Service as a mail carrier, and he has stayed with that job ever since. Vanessa has been a housewife all their married life and has never worked outside her home. Sometimes she takes in sewing to supplement the family income, but for the most part she spends her days taking care of their home, reading and watching television.

It was a great disappointment to them when they learned, three years after they married, that Vanessa was unable to bear children, and for a while they considered adopting a child, but they were frustrated by the long delays and uncertainties involved in adoption. Eventually they settled into a life as a childless couple.

Despite their sadness over this problem, however, their childlessness did give them freedom to travel and, for a time, they were spending much of their income flying all over the country, following Elvis as he traveled on his various concert tours. They found great excitement and joy in seeing Elvis perform, and even to this day they brighten up and become noticeably enthusiastic as they talk about the spectacular shows of the man Harry calls "the world's greatest entertainer."

When Elvis died, it was hard on both of them, but it seemed particularly devastating for Vanessa. Even in March of 1984, she was weeping as she reflected back on her reactions to the events of August 16, 1977.

66When Harry got home from work that day, he hadn't heard about what had happened. I was in my sewing room crying my eyes out when he walked in, and he thought someone in our family had died. At first I couldn't catch my breath long enough to tell him what I was crying about, but finally I stammered, "Elvis is dead."

He said, "Oh, no, what happened?" I told him what I knew and we turned on the radio and television to try to get the latest news.

Nobody knows what a hard year that was for me, that year after Elvis died. Plus, my step-sister died six weeks later. She had been one of my best friends since I was seven years old. After she died I could hardly get out of bed for a month. I would stay in bed and try to sleep and forget it all.

The year after Elvis died, I started daydreaming about him a lot. I would have these little imagined conversations in my head with Elvis. I would ask him what he was doing, and where he was, and things about his life, personal things, mostly, and then I would imagine him giving his answers back to me. I would try to imagine what his voice would sound like as he gave his answers back to me.

This went on for a couple of years. It made me feel better, so I went on doing it, but it did worry me, too. I wondered if I was going crazy, or what. In high school, I used to daydream about Elvis a lot. I would daydream that he and I were friends and he would invite me to come to Graceland and we would ride horses together.

When I met Harry and it became plain that Harry and I were in love, I told him one day, "You will always have to share me with Elvis Presley." He laughed and said that was O.K. with him because he liked Elvis, too. It's funny, but I knew from the moment he said that that Harry was the one for me, because he understood about me loving Elvis.

So later, after I fell in love with Harry, I would have daydreams about Elvis, Harry, and me. I would daydream about us being friends. In the daydream, Harry got a job with Elvis on the sound crew, because Harry has always been good with electronics, and we would travel around with Elvis as he gave concerts.

So those were the daydreams I had in high school. After we got married the daydreams kind of dropped off, I guess, though in a way they came true since we would travel around a lot going to Elvis's concerts.

Then, that year after Elvis died, the daydreams came back. Some days I would spend the better part of the day listening to Elvis records and daydreaming that I was talking with him. It bothered me. It really did. I didn't know if it was normal or not for a grown woman to be having daydreams about Elvis all the time. So finally I brought it up with Harry. I told him I was worried and sad. I told him about the daydreams and I asked him what he thought we should do. **"**

For his part, Harry told me, he was very concerned about his wife's health when he found out what had been happening to her. It had rapidly become obvious to me, as I talked with them, that they are a very loving couple, absolutely dependent upon each other. It was a real strain on Harry to learn about Vanessa's daydreams, he said.

"I was worried to death about Vanessa. Even before she told me about the daydreams, I had felt there was something going on with her because sometimes I would see her staring off into space. Sometimes she wouldn't answer at first when I asked her a question, and I would have to ask her a couple of times before she would hear me. This one night I said, "Vanessa, is there something bothering you?" She told me she had been having spells of daydreaming about talking to Elvis.

I was worried about her, yes, I was. Finally, I even considered taking her to a psychiatrist, but she was so embarrassed and we were both afraid they might try to take her into the mental hospital. Besides, Dr. Moody, and I don't mean this to be any reflection on you, but I have always heard that many psychiatrists are not religious men. Vanessa and I are strong Christians, and I didn't want her to be going to anyone who would try to interfere with our religious faith.

I just didn't know what to do. I thought if there was some way I could get her mind onto something else she might cheer up. Now, at that time I was getting into home computers. I have played around with electronics and radios since I was a boy. I got a home computer as soon as they came out, and now I have several. I subscribe to several home computer magazines and keep up on all the latest things.

One night in 1981 I was in the basement playing around with my computer and it just hit me. I could make up a program where you could ask questions of Elvis and the answers would come back on the screen. It would be kind of like talking with Elvis. I figured Vanessa and I could do it together and we would both get a kick out of it. So I made up a list of twenty-five questions people might like to ask Elvis. I looked through all our old magazines and books about Elvis and I got hundreds of quotes from him. I even went to the Library of Congress and found lots of interviews that had been done with him over the years, and I copied them on a Xerox machine. So for all of the twenty-five questions, I got answers in his own words. Then I wrote a program where you could type in a question and the answer in Elvis's words would come up on the screen and you could read it. I made it up as a surprise for Vanessa. She wondered what I was doing those six weeks, but finally one evening I took her down to the basement to show her. I sat her down at the keyboard of the computer and I said, "Vanessa, type in 'Hello, Elvis, are you there?'" And the answer came back on the screen: "Yes, Vanessa, I am. How are you doing today?"

Well, then I showed her how to work the computer. I showed her the list of twenty-five questions. That first night, we were down in the basement until way past midnight, playing with the Elvis program. And at that stage, it wasn't much. Just twenty-five questions and each one just had a single possible answer.

Later on we wrote more questions and wrote answers which we thought Elvis would probably give, if he were asked. Vanessa helped a lot. Sometimes I would write an answer and she would say, "I don't think Elvis would say it like that. He would probably say. . . ." And she would write what his answer would be like.

It got more complex as we worked on it. For some questions now we have as many as seven or eight answers, and I've got it fixed so that you can't tell which one will come up. You can do it several times and not get the same answer twice. But all of them sound like him.

Vanessa has become a different person since I put Elvis into our computer. She got so interested in this she was cheerful again in just a couple of weeks. I like to play with it, too. We like to say we are the only couple in the world who has Elvis in their home computer. **"**

Eventually, then, what started as a kindhearted attempt on Harry's part to help his wife became an engrossing hobby. Now it has developed into a major preoccupation in their lives. They chatted excitedly as they told me of their plans to go on enlarging their storehouse of answers and to improve their system to make it more and more lifelike. As they talked about their dreams, it was clear that while Harry was the technical wizard of the pair, Vanessa also played an indispensable role in creating the electronic Elvis which was gradually taking shape in their basement. It was her deep feeling for Elvis and her sensitivities to the subtleties of his life, style, and character which imparted a flesh and blood feeling to the conversations which were enacted through the flickering gadgets crammed into Harry's basement study.

Harry beamed as he told me of what he foresaw for the couple's project.

❝Our next step is to get as much footage of real-life filmed interviews with Elvis as we can. Then we will put them all on video tapes and set up the computer so you can type in a question and — zap — there he'll be on the TV screen answering your question. But, Dr. Moody, with the technology that will be available in a few years we'll be able to make something like this that will be amazing. There will be computerized voice synthesizers that will be able to imitate anybody's voice well enough that you can't tell the difference. There will be computerized pictures. You could make pictures from the computer that would look so much like Elvis himself that you would swear they were movies of him. Then you could run the synthesized voice of Elvis through the screen, too, and it would look and sound just like him talking to you through the TV. The possibilities are endless.❞

While Harry's conversation that night tended toward the technical and electronic, Vanessa's words rang with deep human emotion and intuition. As much as Harry loved putting together novel circuitry, Vanessa delighted in interacting with his contrivances. It struck me that she had what I took at the time to be an almost little-girl-like belief in the reality of these electronically simulated interactions with Elvis Presley.

❝The first time I used the computer with Harry's Elvis program, it seemed like a game. But as we worked out new programs they got better all the time and it got more and more real. Now when I go down into the basement I feel almost as though I am really in contact with Elvis. It's so complicated now, you see, that you never can tell exactly what Elvis is going to say next. So it's like you're talking to another person, you just can't see him. Sometimes I get the feeling that he is really down there in the basement, hanging around the computers. It's eerie. It's so eerie I can't go down there and turn on those machines without Harry going down there with me. It's too scary for me to go down there by myself. I get spooked.

At times I actually feel that he really does talk to me through the computer in some way. Sometimes I am convinced that the spirit of Elvis Presley has taken over our computer. **"**

I should make one more observation about Harry and Vanessa. Both of them, though to differing degrees, exemplify a most interesting style of human existence. There are many persons who have a tendency to retire away from others, to keep to themselves, to remain unobtrusive. Persons of this temperament display a remote reserve and are close to only one or two others, usually family members. They may go through life with remarkably little need for close emotional ties with large numbers of other people. They are often drawn to pursuits which involve mathematics and often come up with strikingly creative ideas. Not surprisingly, then, they may be given to daydreaming.

Harry and Vanessa have developed an ideal solution to the problems encountered by persons like this. Deeply engrossed in each other and their relationship with Elvis, they live out their lives, content.

CHAPTER VIII

Moments Frozen In Time: Flashbulb Memories of August 16, 1977

IN APRIL, 1986, I HAD completed and written up the interviews upon which this book is based. I realized at that time that in order better to understand and to interpret the unusual experiences I had uncovered, I needed a broader base of understanding of the public perception of Elvis Presley and of the events surrounding his death. I had been greatly impressed by the fact that almost all of the persons whom I had interviewed had described to me vivid memories of exactly where they had been and what they had been doing the moment they learned of Elvis's death. Were such precise and detailed memories of the event peculiar to the type of people who would also have strange psychic experiences relating to Elvis Presley, I wondered, or, rather, were memories of this kind common among the general population as well?

Accordingly, in that month, I undertook a sort of public opinion survey in hopes of learning more about public

-115-

attitudes and knowledge about Elvis and about his death. I surveyed at random fifty people, men and women alike, thirty to sixty-six years old. All were strangers to me. I approached them at two locations in a small southern city: in a shopping mall and in the waiting room of a metropolitan hospital. I identified myself as a psychiatrist who was writing a book about the reactions of people to Elvis Presley's death.

Five of the persons whom I approached declined to be interviewed. The other forty-five talked freely and openly. Three interesting findings emerged from this survey. All three, I believe, are relevant to the understanding and the interpretation of the unusual psychic experiences reported earlier in this book.

These findings are: first, that a large percentage of the persons whom I approached reported vivid "flashbulb" memories of the moment they heard of Elvis's death; second, that a large percentage of these people seemed to know quite a few details about his life and personality and attributed a large range of highly desirable characteristics to him; and, third (and most amazing), there are apparently a number of people who express serious doubts about the reality of Elvis Presley's death. Let us look at these three findings in turn.

1. The Flashbulb Memories: In April of 1986, almost ten years after the event, twenty-nine of the forty-five people I interviewed could provide me with vivid, detailed recollections of exactly where they were, what they were doing, and how they felt when they heard the news of Elvis Presley's death. Even granted that this survey took place in the South, where Elvis is perhaps more

of a folk hero than he is in other sections of the country, this seems to be a very high percentage.

Memories of this kind — in which a person vividly recalls not only a certain fact, but also where he was and what he was doing when he first learned of the event — are called "flashbulb memories." Although psychologists have a great deal of difficulty explaining them, they seem to be a universal human experience. An older generation of Americans retains such memories about the circumstances they were in when they learned of the bombing of Pearl Harbor. The details of their surroundings and thoughts upon hearing of the assassination of President John F. Kennedy are burned into the memories of many millions of people who are old enough to remember that tragedy. Similarly, I surmise from my research that multitudes of persons have flashbulb memories of hearing about Elvis Presley's death.

All of the memories I collected were vivid and emotionally charged. Many were touching and poignant. Collectively, they indicate that the death of Elvis Presley had an enormous impact on the American psyche.

Kathryn Sams is a high-school English teacher, forty-nine years old. She remembered,

❝I was getting ready to wash the picture window in my living room. The television was on. I walked into the living room with a bottle of window cleaner and a cloth, and just as I sprayed one squirt out of the bottle of window cleaner, the news came on TV. They said Elvis Presley died. I thought it couldn't be. I was so upset I couldn't think straight. I went next door to the neighbor's house to tell her. It upset me so much I couldn't think of cleaning that window. Every time I would think about cleaning the window after that, I would think of Elvis Presley dying, so I would stop. Finally, after I guess three months, I got my daughter to clean it when she came over one day. "

Brenda Cartright, thirty-eight years old, is employed as a physician's assistant. She recalls reporting to work at the hospital where she is employed. She noticed that the atmosphere there seemed gloomy.

"I walked into the emergency room that evening to begin my shift. I could tell right away that something was wrong. All my co-workers were sitting around looking glum. I said, "What's the matter?" The nurse on duty said, "Haven't you heard? Elvis Presley is dead." I was looking right into her face as she said it. It came as a shock. I didn't have any enthusiasm for my work the rest of the evening. When things were slow, we would go back into the working area, behind the front desk, and watch the developments on television.

One of the things I remember about the evening was that one woman, who was hysterical about Elvis's death, was brought in by her family. She had to be sedated. She was there a couple of hours, at least, while the social worker got her calmed down. "

Another vivid recollection came from Curt Willis, a forty-year-old construction contractor/house builder. At the time of Elvis's death, he was employed as a deputy sheriff.

"My partner and I had been called to a real tough neighborhood because of a domestic dispute. When we got there, this couple was just about to kill each other. The woman had the man down and was choking him. We pulled them apart and I was holding onto the man, holding him back, trying to keep him from getting at his wife, and my partner was talking to the woman. Just then, it came over our walkie-talkie unit that Elvis had died. The woman started crying and the man went limp. Both of them were real upset. This seemed to take their attention from their fight and they went to watching TV and talking about Elvis. It was real strange. We left and didn't hear anything more from them that night.**"**

Herbert Billingsley, who is a fifty-eight-year-old chief loan officer at a bank, was on the job when he heard the news.

"One of our customers came into the bank late that afternoon and told us that Elvis Presley was dead. I was shocked. There was a moment there when I didn't believe it. Then I knew it must be true. One of the tellers fell apart when she heard it. She left that night to go to Memphis. She didn't come back to work for several days.**"**

Andy Martin, fifty, is a salesman for a farm equipment company. He says:

"I can tell you exactly where I was. I was driving across the 10th Street Bridge. I was in the middle of the bridge when the news came on the radio. All the announcer said was that Elvis was dead and they would have details later. My first reaction was sadness. Sadness and disbelief. The first thought that came into my mind was, "This is the end of an era." And it's true. Whatever anyone may think of him, Elvis started a whole new way of thinking and a whole new kind of music in this country . . . in the world. 99

Linda Webber, thirty-five, is a church secretary. She recalls:

66That afternoon, my boyfriend took me to a baseball game. We were having fun, but after a while they flashed up on the scoreboard that Elvis Presley was dead. My boyfriend actually yelled. We didn't have the heart to see a baseball game after that. I noticed a lot of people leaving at the same time we got up to leave. I assume most of them were leaving because of Elvis dying. I know the couple who walked out right in front of us were leaving because of Elvis, because the woman was crying and she told me she couldn't stand to be sitting there watching a baseball game with that on her mind. We went out on the street and then took a taxi downtown. My boyfriend went into every record store we could find and started buying up Elvis Presley records. I don't even know how many he ended up buying. A lot. I was sad, but my boyfriend was totally wiped out by the thing. Everywhere we went for the rest of that day, people were crying or telling stories about Elvis. 99

Henry Overton is now sixty-two. He had no trouble at all recalling the events of that day in August 1977.

"I remember it well because I am the manager of a grocery store and pandemonium broke loose in the store on the day when Elvis died. A woman came running in all out of breath and told some of the other shoppers, whom she knew, about it, and pretty soon it was all over the store. One of my check-out clerks passed out and we had to send her home. I was scared somebody was going to be hurt in all the rushing and confusion that was going on and we would be sued. After a while, nobody came into the store. That was just as well, because I couldn't get a lick of work out of most of the employees the rest of that day. Everyone was feeling so bad about Elvis.**"**

Lily Hunnicutt is now retired from her job as a military pay clerk. She is in her late sixties.

"I had worked hard in my garden all day long and my muscles were sore. I came in and filled up the bathtub with hot water and I got in to soak. I turned on the radio to listen to some music, and it was right then I heard that Elvis had died. I cried, I really did, and I felt lonely. You know, I didn't feel like getting up from that tub. I sat there for two hours soaking and listening to the radio as they played Elvis's songs. When I finally got out, I felt so bad I had to take a sleeping pill to get to sleep at all that night.**"**

Rod Shields, a fifty-year-old psychology professor, who had been a professional musician with a rock 'n' roll band in the fifties, provided me with a particularly graphic account of this type. His words vibrantly and incisively capture the peculiar, nostalgic alteration in the state of consciousness which typically accompanies flash-bulb memories.

66I remember being at a state park. A friend of mine and I were out hiking. He had a radio with him and over the news came the event that Elvis Presley had died. I just sort of stopped in my tracks and my friend continued to walk and then he stopped. I began to kind of go back into a lot of remembering, flashes of the fifties, and particularly myself in Los Angeles, playing rock 'n' roll music and listening to Elvis records and how much I identified with the music.

It was very vivid. The memories were very vivid. There was a real emotional feeling about the music. It seemed to really move me at the time. I felt this sense of loss, a real sense of loss when I heard this. I felt so shocked, and stopped in my tracks. This message had somehow stopped time for me, and I entered this other world of the past. As this feeling began to sort of fade away, I seemed to come back to the present in a new way, actually. I felt my feet on the ground, I noticed the sunlight coming through the trees. I felt all there, very in the present.

Obviously, this was a break in my mundane world, a break in my routine way of doing things or taking things for granted. It had shaken me. Nothing could change what had happened. Nothing could be done. It was final, all over, final. Because of that finalness, it seemed to relate to an experience of complete letting go.

It wasn't like I was depressed. There was a kind of feeling of unreality to it. This is what life is all about. These things suddenly break in at any moment. And here was an individual that had a great deal of influence in my past, and he was gone. I felt sadness, and yet, a real appreciation of having been left with this music, and a realization that it would not go away.

I was mostly silent. I didn't talk to my friend. Most of these things were taking place within my own experiencing. **"**

Memories like these, I presume, haunt millions of people all over the world. Also, it appears that, in this regard, the persons whose stories of unusual psychic experiences involving Elvis Presley were reported in earlier chapters of this book are not any different from the normal population. That is, the fact that a large proportion of the persons reporting these experiences also describe vivid flashbulb memories relating to Elvis's death in itself does not make them any different from the population at large.

2. "What Elvis Meant To Me" — Results Of A Survey: I also asked the persons who participated in the survey about what characteristics they attributed to Elvis as a person, and — if they admired him — what it was about him that most impressed them. This would be helpful, I felt, because in gathering the psychic experiences reported earlier, I had noticed that the persons who told me of the experiences attributed an exceptionally broad range of characteristics to the singer. I wondered whether this tendency was specific to persons whose frame of mind was such that they would also produce unusual psychic experiences related to Elvis, or whether, instead, members of the general population attributed these same characteristics to Elvis.

Altogether, in the public opinion survey I conducted, no fewer than fifteen characteristics were attributed to Elvis Presley by the persons whom I interviewed. These characteristics were (1) kindness, warmth and sincerity ("He was a sweet person, very nice."); (2) generosity ("He was always giving cars to people he met on the street."); (3) success ("He was a poor boy who made good."); (4) material wealth (He "was rich," "had a palace," "had a fleet of cars," "could get all the money he wanted," etc.); (5) being a good son ("He was real close to his mother." "I hear he hired his father to be his business manager."); (6) humor ("He was funny on stage." "He could laugh at himself."); (7) sadness ("He got into trouble with drugs." "He couldn't handle it when his mother died."); (8) macho ("I read where he broke up a fight at a filling station once." "He was good at karate."); (9) fun-loving ("He knew how to have a good time."); (10) a great entertainer ("He had a wonderful voice." "He put on a good show."); (11) influence on others ("None of this, the Beatles, rock music, generally, could have gone anywhere without him."); (12) loyalty to his friends ("I hear he took good care of his friends.); (13) sex appeal ("When I think of Elvis, I think of sex."); (14) law and order ("He was all in favor of America, I know that." "I believe President Nixon made him an officer for drug enforcement."); and (15) strong religious faith ("He was a convinced Christian." "I like his gospel songs best. You can tell he sang them from the heart.").

In conducting these interviews, I was impressed with the degree of detail in which many people apparently knew his life history, and how easily and colorfully they could relate particular anecdotes about him.

It was also obvious to me that the list of characteristics attributed to Elvis by participants in the public opinion survey coincided with the characteristics attributed to him by the persons who had unusual psychic experiences related to Elvis. Here again, then, the persons who had these experiences did not seem different, as a group, from the general population in the way they perceived Elvis.

By far the most fascinating result of my survey, however, came as a complete surprise. I found that some people refuse to believe that Elvis is dead.

3. The Elvis Conspiracy: "You don't really believe that Elvis Presley is dead, do you?" Charles Lassiter asked me, arching one eyebrow in a somewhat condescending manner, as he spoke. His question came in response to mine; I had just asked him what his reactions to Elvis's death had been. I was surprised and puzzled by Charles's query. He had anticipated my confusion and needed no further prompting to elaborate.

66Right now, I'm not saying I really believe this happened, that Elvis really died. Because so much has happened in the last few years. I still can't say I believe he is dead because there are so many things that happen today. So many people say they are dead that are not dead. I can't say for sure, in my mind, that Elvis is dead.

I just can't believe it, I can't. It's funny, but I can't. You hear people saying that someone is dead, and then you find out they're not dead, but they left the country. Elvis may have decided to move away, to get some relief and enjoy himself. **"**

As startling as my encounter with Charles and his unusual belief was, I have since discovered that he is only one of a veritable army of true believers who, against all the evidence and in defiance of common sense, still refuse to believe that the death of Elvis Presley is fact.

Bobby Smith, a friend of mine who has had a long career in the music business, gave me an extended and lively account of how this bizarre willingness to believe that Elvis was still alive came into play on an international scale in the late 1970's and early 1980's. During that period, Bobby managed a popular singer who appeared under the stage name of "Orion." Orion performed wearing a mask and bore a certain superficial physical resemblance to Elvis Presley. His voice was also nearly identical to that of the late singer. When he burst on the national scene, around the time of Elvis's death, an amazing craze developed among multitudes of people in the United States and Europe. Actively encouraged and abetted by sensational articles in popular national magazines and newspapers, many thousands of people came to believe that Elvis had staged his own death, then started a new career as the masked singer, Orion. Despite vigorous assertions to the contrary from the singer and from his perplexed manager, countless people continued to believe (as many still do) that Orion was secretly Elvis Presley. Bobby's lucid descriptions of his sense of awe as he witnessed this incredible spectacle taking place before his own eyes can hardly be bested.

❝I had a recording studio in Brunswick, Georgia, in 1977, when some people I knew brought in an unknown young singer for an audition. I listened to him, and, of course, at that time Elvis was still alive, and I said, "I can't use you. You sound too much like Elvis. I would never have anything to do with an imitator."

And the guy says, "Well, I'm not an imitator. This is me."

I said, "Well, I can't sell records on you with that kind of voice."

So, anyway, the people stayed and we went out that night with the young singer to a little nightclub called The Lighthouse, on St. Simon's Island. Some of the musicians who worked at my studio played in this club at night, so we stopped by there. They called him up to sing and he got up there and I'm telling you, the people in that club went crazy. They were hollering for more when he finally came down off the stage.

The next day, I took the young man to my studio and I told my engineer, "Take different songs in different keys and put his voice on them back in the studio, and bring them back to me. If he's an imitator, I'll find out, because, with these different songs, it will show up." My engineer did this, and he came back to me.

He shook his head and he said, "Bobby, these are all the same."

So the young singer was not an imitator. So I signed him to a five-record contract. After the first record was released, Elvis passed on, and that kind of opened the door for him. We adopted the name Orion for him and we came up with the idea of the mask.

Then articles started appearing in magazines — "Is Elvis Still Alive?" and "The King Is Alive: Mystery Singer

Is Really Elvis." It made it hard for Orion, because no matter what anybody wrote about him, they would not write an article without mentioning Elvis's name, and Orion didn't like that. When people would ask about it, he would say, "I'm not Elvis, I'm Orion."

Yet anybody could look at him, even in the mask, and tell that Orion is not Elvis. He wore no Elvis outfits on the stage, and he didn't sing Elvis songs in his shows. He wore his own outfits and sang his own songs.

Still, people believed. People actually believed that Orion was Elvis. People would even come up to me at the concerts and say that Orion has a scar on his throat at such and such a place, and Elvis had one there, too. They would come to me comparing all kinds of scars, the same this, the same that.

I never will forget one night at one of the concerts, a lady who was convinced that Orion was Elvis leaned over to me as we were standing near Orion, and she said, "He looks so good. Is he all right? Is his health all right?"

They really, really believed. We would pull up in that Silver Eagle bus of his we toured in, and when they found out what hotel we were going to be at, the parking lot would be filled up with people with cameras, all believing that he was Elvis. When he would get off that bus, people would faint. He had a following that was as big as many of the superstars, I mean die-hard fans that would drive five hundred, a thousand miles to see him in concert, and stand in line in the rain to buy tickets. People even came from England to see him.

A lot of psychics wrote that Orion was definitely Elvis. At concerts, you would have to see it to believe it, the people who would line up for autographs and just stare at him and take pictures. They wanted to believe it. The diehard Elvis fans wanted to believe it. People would bring their little children for him to hold, believing he was Elvis. People would mob him.

They really wanted to believe that he was Elvis. I think Elvis had such a following and people loved him so much because he was the one that changed rock 'n' roll, and I think that people didn't want to accept his death. And Orion was like a new hope for them. They would believe whatever they wanted to believe, you know.

Orion wanted to get away from the mask and be himself, and when that happened, his career fell down. Because then the people's dream, that they thought he was Elvis, the die-hards that really believed it, they didn't want to know anything else. When he took the mask off, then it just wasn't the same. The electricity wasn't there. Not that any of us ever tried to say that he was Elvis or anything. We never did that, and we denied it.

People just didn't want to accept the fact that Elvis was dead. Orion still sells records everywhere, even in Europe. Some people still won't accept that he is not Elvis, even yet. They still believe.**"**

Why should people cling so tenaciously to such improbable doctrines and peculiar fantasies? In the following, concluding chapter, I will try to shed some light on the human meaning of such behavior, and on its relationship to the strange psychic experiences which were detailed earlier in this book.

CHAPTER IX

Conclusion:
Mourning Becomes
Elvis

MY RESEARCH INDICATES that there must be hundreds of people who, around the time of his death or afterwards, had psychic experiences involving Elvis Presley. How are we to understand this? And is there anything of significance to be learned through a study of these events?

On one level, of course, such stories are fascinating, even eerie and disturbing, and it is for this reason that bizarre happenings involving Elvis frequently crop up as part of the standard fare of the weekly tabloid newspapers. To dwell on the sensational aspects of these touchingly human accounts, however, is to ignore their deeper meaning. For, placed in proper perspective, these tales have a lot to tell us about the psychology of psychic experiences.

Typically, studies of psychic experiences are of two distinct, supposedly contrasting types. In one type, a sympathetic investigator gathers reports of purported paranormal experiences, analyzes them, gives reasons why they cannot be explained away as instances of known natural phenomena, and concludes that these experiences "prove" or "give evidence for" the existence of supernatural forces not understood by contemporary science. In the second type, a skeptical, often ornery investigator takes reports of alleged paranormal happenings and tries systematically to debunk them by explaining them away, by showing, in effect, that they are simply instances of known natural or psychological phenomena.

Although studies of these two types are commonly regarded as being in direct opposition to each other, in fact, from a broader perspective, both approaches have a great deal in common. The most obvious common feature is the notion that the ultimate purpose of the investigator of supposed paranormal experiences must be to determine whether or not the experiences are "real."

The passage of time reveals, overall, how fruitless this debate has been. Confirmed debunkers of and confirmed believers in psychic phenomena have been locked, it appears, in a dusty stalemate for decades. Proponents of both sides in this drama seem to have a vested interest in their own respective points of view. The result has been that an important dimension of experience, one which holds an inexhaustible fascination for the human mind, has somehow gotten lost amidst the fury of a battle between conflicting ideologies. Unfortunately, what is commonly missing in studies of both types is any sort of sympathetic exploration of the emotional context of psychic experiences.

By giving up the artificial requirement that a study of purported psychic experiences must have as its aim either to "prove" or to "disprove" the "reality" of psychic experiences, one can approach them in a much more balanced fashion and can comfortably explore their human meaning.

As I stated in the Introduction, the passage of time since the experiences with which this book deals and the fact that the reports are entirely anecdotal in nature, deriving from fallible human memory, make it obvious that, especially at this late date, the "reality" of these experiences can be neither proven nor disproven. This does not mean that they were unreal; it means only that we cannot prove either alternative. Even given this stricture, however, there is a great deal we can say about these experiences.

The first point I would like to make is that the people who reported these experiences were not psychotic, *i.e.*, "crazy." This is important because in the context of our culture, persons who publicly report unusual states of consciousness of this nature must brace themselves against being perceived or labelled as "crazy." In fact, though, in my experience and in that of many other investigators, people who report psychic experiences are typically not psychotic and indeed may be quite sane and well-balanced. Psychic or paranormal experiences may be considered aberrant in our society, but they are aberrant in a very different way from the way in which psychotic experiences are.

Interestingly enough, over the years I have encountered quite a few psychotic persons who have seized upon the image of Elvis Presley, making him a central fixation in their own particular madness. It is relevant here to describe a few of these unfortunate individuals who are literally "crazy about Elvis" in order to illustrate how different psychotic experience is, in general, from psychic experience.

Psychosis is an extreme form of mental illness in which the affected person's ability to communicate with others, to behave appropriately, to think, and to interpret reality is so grossly disordered that he or she is unable to meet the ordinary demands of daily living. The main forms of psychosis are schizophrenia, paranoia, and mania; and, as far as we can tell, psychotic illnesses of the types we know today have occurred among human beings at least since the dawn of history.

However, interesting changes have occurred in the *content* of psychotic experience. In the medieval period the delusions and fixations of many psychotic persons had to do with religious figures and images. While many psychotic persons today still develop religious fixations (for example, I have encountered quite a few disturbed persons over the years who suffer from the delusional conviction that they are God, or Christ, or the Virgin Mary), in more recent times, many psychotics also can be found who incorporate more modern imagery into their illnesses. Hence, when scientists began to discover various kinds of invisible rays, and when radio and television broadcasting was developed, bringing with it wide public dissemination of theories of various kinds of electromagnetic radiation, many psychotic persons began to develop delusional beliefs to the effect that they were being bombarded with various kinds of mysterious "rays," or that their minds were being controlled by radiation being beamed at them by sinister organizations.

Within the past few decades, many psychiatrists have also seen a growing number of mentally disordered people whose strange beliefs and bizarre behavior revolves around various rock singers. I once worked on a ward in a mental hospital in which all of the patients were severely psychotic, many violent. During one period, there were two different patients there at the same time, each of whom was convinced that he was the rock singer Michael Jackson. This kind of delusion is so common that I am sure there must be large numbers of psychiatrists who can relate similar examples.

Over the years, I have encountered an amazing number of psychotic persons who were obsessed with Elvis in one way or another. I remember a woman in her mid-fifties who developed a condition called de Clerambault's syndrome, or erotomania. The victim of this syndrome is typically a woman who becomes obsessed with the belief that an older, prominent male (often a nationally known celebrity or a respected citizen in her community) is in love with her. Victims of de Clerambault's syndrome can talk of little else than their delusion. They may send the object of their affections letter after letter and often become convinced that he is sending them secret messages of love through his television appearances. When they are spurned by their beloved (who are almost universally bewildered and alarmed by these advances), they sometimes become violent, even assaultive, toward the person whom they claim they love.

The woman I mentioned developed this syndrome when she was thirty-five years old. Ever since, she can think and talk of little else other than Elvis; her fixation has so interfered with her life that she cannot function in any normal context of life. Whatever one says to her about any subject whatsoever, she immediately associates the remark with Elvis and brings the conversation back to him at once. When he died, she was devastated; she moved to Memphis to live near his grave and still maintains the belief that he was secretly in love with her (even though she never even once met him face-to-face).

I know of many other cases in which the inner lives of psychotic persons revolve around the imaginary Elvises of their minds. I remember a young woman in her mid-twenties who was hospitalized for the treatment of severe disturbance. Throughout her hospital stay, she remained convinced that at any moment Elvis and his entourage would swoop down from the sky in helicopters, storm the mental hospital where she was confined, rescue her, and fly her back to Graceland, where she would join Elvis's staff as an assistant. Once, when repairs were being made on some of the rooms in an adjoining ward, she became severely agitated and interpreted the loud noises coming from the workmen's construction tools as Elvis and his band trying to batter down the walls of the hospital in order to break in and release her. Whenever the noise of a plane was heard overhead, she concluded that Elvis was about to arrive on his mission.

Another middle-aged woman of my acquaintance, who is chronically psychotic, regularly becomes convinced, during the acute exacerbations of her illness, that she is pregnant with Elvis Presley's child. She must be admitted to the hospital and confined in the psychotic ward because her relatives are unable to manage her at home during these crises. While she is in the hospital, she eventually experiences mock labor (even showing apparent labor contractions). So delivered of her "baby for Elvis," she is able to be discharged to the care of her family until she develops another of her phantom pregnancies. Such false pregnancies (the condition is called pseudocyesis) are fairly common; what makes this particular example unusual is simply the patient's delusion that Elvis is the father of the supposed infant.

I could describe other cases. I know of a young man who is tormented by a voice in his head. This symptom, as such, is not rare; indeed, hallucinated voices are a common symptom of schizophrenia. However, in this case, the voice the young man hears is that of Elvis Presley. He cannot escape the voice; he hears it constantly. Since he will talk of nothing else but the voice in his head, his friends have withdrawn from him. He lives in a state of never-ending perplexity and loneliness.

In a town in which I once lived, there is another man, now approaching early middle age, who sits all day in a public park, his hair style and dress modeled after those of Elvis. He plays tapes of Elvis Presley's music on a portable tape player. He stares ahead impassively, his eyes glazed. Sometimes he mouths the words of the songs. Somewhere, deep in the recesses of his mind, he believes that he *is* Elvis.

Yet another man is obsessed with wondering why God made Elvis, and not him, Elvis. "Why," he asks again and again, "did God make Elvis Elvis, and not me?" His obsession interferes with his life; he remains unhappy and nonfunctional. I'm sure that many psychiatrists could add to this list.

In all these cases, and, no doubt, many others like them, the fixation with Elvis interferes with the ability of these persons to communicate with others, to live integrated and fulfilled lives, to think, to deal with reality. These people are, in truth, psychotic, "crazy about Elvis."

When it comes to the psychic experiences with which I have dealt, however, we do not see the kind of loss of ability to deal with reality and disorganization of the personality which are present is the lives of the psychotic persons I have described. By and large, the persons with whom I have talked who report psychic experiences related to Elvis are functional; no psychotic disturbances are present, and, on the whole, these persons are in good contact with reality.

It seems to me fruitless to search in the realm of the major psychoses to find known psychological phenomena which match up with the unusual mental events which have been described in earlier chapters of this volume. However, there is a well-studied psychological process which, when it is disturbed or goes awry, sometimes results in states of mind which, though bizarre, are not frankly psychotic in nature. I am referring to the constellation of mental events, feelings, images, and functions which is activated in response to the death of a significant other. The psychological literature concerning grief and bereavement is rife with descriptions of phenomena which closely resemble the psychic experiences concerning Elvis Presley with which I have been dealing. Some of the widely reported manifestations of grief and bereavement are: shock and numbing, denial, sadness, preoccupation with the image of the deceased, taking on the characteristics of the deceased, psychosomatic disturbances, establishing a "shrine" for the departed person, and "anniversary reactions." Following are explanations of these states.

1. Shock and Numbing — Perhaps the most common response of a human being who first learns of the death of a beloved other person is a state of shock or numbing. Very often, when people are describing how they felt when they learned of the death of a significant other, they resort to phrases such as, "I was shocked," or, "I felt numb." Photographs taken on the scene of disasters in which large numbers of persons were killed and others survived capture this state graphically. Such photographs often show uninjured survivors sitting around with blank stares on their faces, apparently numbed and unable to move.

2. Denial — Typically, people who learn of the death of a loved one say, "I just can't believe it," "It can't be," or other words to that effect. It's not that they don't know; deep down, they do. Denial in this sense is a psychological defense mechanism. The knowledge that his or her loved one is dead is barred from the conscious mind so as to keep the terrible pain of the loss from being felt so acutely. Sometimes such denial goes on for extreme lengths of time after death. I once had as a patient a middle-aged man whose wife had died some months before; he was so overwhelmed by the loss that he denied it and continued to assert (and consciously believe) that she was alive and was out of town visiting relatives.

3. Sadness — This is plainly a common part of the mourning process. Bereaved persons may feel sad and have frequent spells of tearfulness, for months, and sometimes years and decades, after the loss of someone they love.

4. Preoccupation with the Image of the Deceased — Bereaved persons may continue to "see" the person who has died for some time after the actual death. A woman whose seven-year-old daughter died related the following to me:

❝One week later, I was walking along the sidewalk in front of my apartment building, and I saw my daughter on the other side of the street. She was surrounded by a beautiful light. It seemed to come from within. She smiled at me, and I knew that she was all right. From then on, I felt much better about her death.**❞**

So many widows have described to me seeing apparitions of their deceased husbands that I could fill an entire book simply with experiences of that type.

For example, one woman described to me an experience that occurred some months after her husband died:

❝My nephew was driving me for an outing in the country. I looked out the window of the car and I saw my husband. He was standing in front of a little house by a lake. He was looking toward me, as though he was expecting someone. I think he was waiting for me.**❞**

The bereft also report frequent dreams in which the deceased person is experienced as still being alive. Or, more concretely, they may carry around and constantly gaze at photographs of the person who has died.

Sometimes people who have such experiences may say that they believe the experience of seeing the deceased person was an illusion, or a dream. Other times, they may believe that they really did see the spirit of the departed. In either case, I wish to emphasize, these experiences are not psychotic. Abundant recent research indicates that seeing apparitions of recently deceased persons is so common and frequent among the bereaved that we can accept it as a normal phase of mourning.

5. Taking on the Characteristics of the Deceased — Very frequently, when someone dies, another member of that person's family may take on some characteristics of the departed person. A psychiatrist recently provided me with an excellent personal example of this phenomenon.

This physician told me that while he had never worn a mustache, his father had always done so. His father died, and some weeks later, as he was preparing to go to work one morning, he shaved as he usually did. However, when he arrived at work, he realized that he had neglected to shave above his lips. Unconsciously, he realized, he had been attempting to keep a little part of his father alive.

There are many examples of this. Very often, other family members will be amazed when a bereaved person begins to imitate the behavior, attitudes, or idiosyncrasies of a family member who has recently died.

6. Psychosomatic Disturbances — There is a high frequency of psychosomatic illness among persons who are in mourning. Digestive disturbances seem to be particularly common among the bereft. Sometimes the bodily disturbances mimic the symptoms of the illness from which the departed person died.

For example, I know of a case of a young man who had to be rushed to the emergency room with chest pains several times during the year following the death of his father from a heart attack. It was clearly established that the chest pains were psychosomatic in nature and that he had no heart disease. The pains were a manifestation of his grief for his father.

7. Establishing a "Shrine" for the Departed Person — Sometimes the family of a person who dies may leave that person's belongings and room undisturbed for months, even decades. This signifies that they cannot let go of the departed person. Objects which belonged to the person who died are, in effect, imbued with something of the identity of that person. They are revered, even made holy.

8. "Anniversary Reactions" — Unusual physical or emotional disturbances are common among the bereaved on poignant anniversaries which are associated with the deceased person: the birthday of the person, for instance, or the anniversary of the person's death. If the connection with the death is not known, the case may seem highly puzzling, even mysterious.

One autumn evening (October 12) I was called to the emergency room of a hospital to see a forty-three-year-old woman who had come in because of difficulty breathing. She had been examined thoroughly by the internal medicine doctors on call, and they could find no plausible physical explanation for her pronounced respiratory distress. Finding her in apparently good physical health, they suspected an emotional basis for the symptoms and called me to interview her. I probed at length but could not find any overt emotional difficulty. I learned that she had never married and lived with her brothers and sisters on the family farm. Flipping through her old hospital record, I happened to notice that she had presented herself at the hospital once before, two years earlier to the day, with the same mysterious symptoms, and that on that occasion, too, the doctors had found no organic basis for her illness. When I asked whether her parents were still alive, she replied that her father had died soon after she was born and that her mother had died three years earlier, on October 12, of pneumonia. The woman had no conscious idea of the connection between her symptoms and her mother's death.

Anniversary reactions are so striking that some of them have passed into the common lore of our society. Sometimes anniversary reactions are so pronounced that persons actually may die on the anniversary of emotionally significant events. Hence, we learn that Thomas Jefferson and John Adams died within hours of each other on July 4, 1826, the fiftieth anniversary of the signing of the Declaration of Independence.

Now that we have looked at some of the common features of bereavement, let us go over them again, this time focusing on the various unusual experiences relating to Elvis Presley which have been described in this book and seeing how certain features of the psychic experiences echo some of the common features of bereavement.

1. Shock and Numbing — Many of the persons who described psychic experiences related to Elvis Presley remarked that they responded with a sense of shock to the news of his death. In addition, however, it seems to me that a consideration of this sense of shock as an almost universal initial response to the unexpected loss of a loved one can give us a novel approach to understanding the experiences of people who reported that they seemed to have some kind of foreknowledge of Elvis's death.

Remember that at the conclusion of the chapter which dealt with such experiences, I remarked that in one way they were not so surprising. For, given that millions of people felt attached to Elvis, and that in the last years of his life it was well known that he was ill and was in and out of hospitals, and that everyone knew that he did not take very good care of his health, it is quite natural that millions of people during that time would be concerned about his health. On any one day during that period, it would be plausible to suppose that thousands of his fans would have passing thoughts or dreams about his death. On the day on which he died, persons who had had such thoughts during the previous few days or even weeks might feel as though these thoughts were uncanny foretellings of the event.

However, there is more to it than that, I believe. Mere coincidence of this nature does not account adequately for the *intensity* with which the psyche of a person who has such an experience seizes upon what happened to him or her as a genuine foretelling of the death. We can better understand this depth of conviction, I submit, if we consider experiences of this type to be, at least in part, an attempt by the mind to deal with the terrible pain which attends the shock of learning about the death of a loved one.

What I am contending is that the pain one feels upon hearing of the death of a significant other is so immense that there is a tendency for acutely grieving persons to seize upon passing thoughts or dreams about the death of the deceased person as a way of attenuating the shock. Obviously, one cannot feel so shocked and so numb if one "knew it all along." Hence, at the moment when one hears the news that a loved person has died, one may be reminded that, a few days before, one had dreamed or thought about that person's dying. This may indeed lessen the shock; one may feel less numbed than one would otherwise. However, the price paid to diminish the shock in this fashion is that one must experience one's previous thought or dream of the person's death in an "uncanny" way, as a "precognition."

2. Denial — Many of the persons I interviewed recalled that initially they "could not believe" that Elvis was dead. This is perfectly normal as an initial response to hearing that someone has died, but when it is maintained for weeks or months or years, it is considered to be pathological.

The people who maintain that the singer Orion is Elvis Presley are, for the most part, engaged in denial. Rumors that Elvis is still alive, having staged his own death and retired away to Hawaii to live, are believed because of the psychological defense of denial. That these beliefs are defensive in nature is suggested by the strange pieces of "evidence" which believers sometimes adduce to support their conviction that Elvis is not dead.

I have heard of several people who are in agreement with one woman who told me that she believes that Elvis is still alive because,

"The date they say Elvis died on is August 16, 1977. Now, the numbers of that date are 8/16/1977, and if you add them up, you get 2001. That is the name of the music he used as his theme song the last few years of his life. So that's just too much to be a coincidence. I'm sure they set that up. Elvis is not dead."

Others who are of this unlikely persuasion point out that since the letters E-L-V-I-S, when rearranged, spell L-I-V-E-S, we can be certain that Elvis is still around somewhere, albeit in hiding, presumably so that he can at last enjoy the benefits of his success, protected now from the constant intrusions which had become a part of his life.

As bizarre as such beliefs are, thousands of persons have entertained them, and some still do. What is more, as strange as they seem, they are closely connected with the perfectly normal, indeed almost universal, sentiment of acute grief which is expressed by phrases like, "I can't believe it."

The manner in which the more florid developments of pathological mourning can arise by almost imperceptible gradations from this common expression of denial, so typical of acute grief, is illustrated beautifully when we place the remarks of Charles Lassiter, quoted in the previous chapter, in their broader context. Charles said, "I can't say for sure, in my mind, that Elvis is dead. I just can't believe it, I can't. . . . You hear people saying that someone is dead, and then you find out they're not dead, but they left the country. Elvis may have decided to move away, to get some relief and enjoy himself."

Here, he obviously vacillates widely from the normal "I just can't believe it," to the bizarre belief that Elvis is still alive, having flown the country to bask in the sun in some foreign clime.

3. Sadness — Several of the persons with whom I talked mentioned a mood of sadness which they had around the time of Elvis's death, or which permeated their experiences.

4. Preoccupation with the Image of the Deceased — The experiences of those who saw "apparitions" of Elvis following his death are identical with the kinds of experiences reported so widely by bereaved widows and other close relatives of deceased persons. Polly Tyson's account of seeing the face of Elvis on her door and Vannessa Grant's imaginary conversations with Elvis also involve the kind of preoccupation with the image of the deceased which is commonly found among the bereaved.

5. Taking on the Characteristics of the Deceased — There is no clear example of this to be found among the cases I have gathered, but the phenomenon of the Elvis imitator is an excellent example. At the recent celebration of the Statue of Liberty in New York, several hundred of these remarkable persons performed simultaneously as part of the festivities. One well-known Elvis impersonator has compared himself to a priest by saying that, just as the priest gives a "live performance" of the presence of Christ, so does the Elvis impersonator give a "live performance" of the presence of Elvis, who is no longer with us "here on earth."

6. Psychosomatic Disturbances — Polly Tyson describes how her health was impaired following Elvis's death, and Harold Welch reports awaking from his dream encounter with Elvis with a headache. Jack Matthews was undergoing physical signs of withdrawal from alcohol, Bess Carpenter was delirious from the effects of an anesthetic, and Lynn Harper seemed to be suffering a temporal lobe seizure during their respective experiences involving Elvis. Such reported effects lead me to believe that an evaluation of the physical health of persons who have uncanny experiences may at times be useful in understanding the experience.

7. **Establishing a Shrine for the Deceased Person** — Elvis's mansion at Graceland has been turned into a national shrine for him, but many other private shrines have been established for him as well. I know of a woman who has had a detailed, life-like, full-sized mannequin of Elvis made. Every year, it is the centerpiece of a spectacular display of Christmas decorations around her home. Ruth Bennett's collection of Elvis records, Marian and Arthur Parker's display of Elvis bric-a-brac, and even Janice McMichael's haunted jacket are examples of private shrines. There must be literally thousands of these treasured collections of mementos. At national gatherings of Elvis Presley fans, such souvenirs are auctioned off on a regular basis, sometimes for sums that would strike outside observers as preposterous.

Based on my own observations of persons who imbue objects associated with Elvis with an almost magical significance, I will hazard a guess that Graceland has probably been a frequent site of mysterious psychic experiences involving Elvis. Although I have no direct word on this, it seems plausible that numbers of people visiting there at one time or another would have reported uncanny happenings similar to those I have recorded.

8. "Anniversary Reactions" — Some of the experiences reported in this book took place around the time of poignant anniversaries associated with Elvis's death. Thus, Polly Tyson was struck by the fact that she first saw the image of the singer on her pantry door within a few days of his birthday, January 8. Similarly, part of the reason Nancy Morgan came to believe that Jeremy was Elvis reincarnated, apparently, was that he was born around the anniversary of the singer's death.

If my thesis that these psychic experiences relating to Elvis are in part a manifestation of mourning is correct, then I would predict that the approaching tenth anniversary of his death probably will give rise to a new spurt of these experiences.

I now want to believe that these experiences with the psychology of mourning also relate to the psychology of our relationships with celebrities. In our modern world, we have succeeded in creating an environment in which we are bombarded with a constant stream of messages from the electronic and print media. One of the means by which we try to impose some sort of order on the flux and flow of information which pervades our world is that of creating celebrities. We focus on particular individuals in this constant stream and collectively see them as exemplars of particular traits, good or bad, which we then admire or condemn them for. Then, by a psychosocial process which in my opinion is still very poorly understood, the media somehow engender in us the illusion that we *know* these individuals.

Our relationships with celebrities differ in many ways from our day-to-day relationships with persons in our immediate environment. The most important difference in the present context is that our relationships with celebrities are far more susceptible to being idealized. If I live every day with another person, I am far more likely to be affected directly not only by his or her good features but also by his or her bad ones. The give-and-take of everyday interaction almost assures that I will come up against the rough edges of the personality of any person with whom I am directly involved.

When it comes to the persons whom we "know" only through their being celebrities, however, the situation is entirely different. In this case, the relationship is, in a remarkable way, asymmetrical. We know them, but they do not know us. This enables us to keep celebrities at a safe emotional distance, however much we choose to imagine that we would really like to be in an everyday, face-to-face, flesh-and-blood relationship with them. The relationships which we imagine in our heads with celebrities can remain forever pure, forever loving, forever free of strife.

Elvis, furthermore, is not just a celebrity; he is a super-celebrity. It has been pointed out that his story bears remarkable parallels to that of the Greek god Orpheus (Dionysius), who was the son of a mighty river and of the sun, and who made magnificent music, and whose appearance drove his female followers into such a frenzy that they ripped pieces of flesh from his body.

Similarly, Elvis was a musician, closely identified with a mighty river (the Mississippi), who made his appearance through Sun Records. Vernon Presley, Elvis's father, among many others, expressed his concern for the way in which his devoted followers would mob him, sometimes leaving him bleeding in the wake of their excited attempts to embrace him.

Or, others may say, Elvis exemplifies the legend of the *puer aeternus*, the perpetual adolescent, as described by the psychiatrist C. G. Jung. The man who typifies the *puer aeternus* is closely connected, as Elvis was, to his mother, and he is a "high liver," seeking out experiences for their sheer excitement. This is very reminiscent of Elvis, who was well known for his love of fancy cars and motorcycles and exciting games and amusements.

But whatever the precise content of the legend, it is plain that Elvis has become, in the modern world, a figure of almost mythic proportion. Indeed, in some of the experiences I have considered, he is elevated almost to the stature of a religious being.

It is wise to keep in mind that Elvis Presley was, after all is said and done, only human. Ultimately, and a bit paradoxically, it was precisely his human features — his vulnerability, his humor, his kindness and generosity — that made him most endearing.

It should be noted that the phenomenon I have been describing is not an exclusively American one. Just as Elvis was admired all over the world, so have experiences like the ones I have reported been reported in other parts of the world. When I was in Europe on a lecture tour in the spring of 1983, I read press accounts of a local psychic who reported fantastic encounters with the ghost of Elvis Presley, and friends have recently forwarded to me reports of the apparition of Elvis being sighted on the stage of a nightclub in Germany.

Furthermore, I am confident that a book similar to this one could be written about other significant national losses — the assassination of President John Kennedy, before Elvis's death, and, after it, the Challenger disaster. Indeed, it has been widely reported that one of America's most beloved comedians, several months before the event, while lying in a dreamy state on a beach and unaccountably even to himself, wrote in his notebook that Kennedy would be assassinated in November. Similarly, an internationally renowned religious leader has said that on the day of the assassination he was troubled by a foreboding that something terrible was about to happen. When he heard the news while on a golf course, he took it as a confirming event.

Already I have heard reports from two people who say that, moments before the liftoff of the doomed spaceship, they were seized with an uncanny awareness that the rocket would explode. A therapist acquaintance of mine has provided me with a case report of a blind friend of his who heard a terrific explosion in his head while sitting in a restaurant. Later, when he heard news reports of the Challenger explosion, he realized that there had been an exact coincidence in the time of the two events and believes that he had been somehow psychically aware of the disaster.

So there should be no dearth of case reports of phenomena such as I have described, whether concerning Elvis or other poignant losses which have been felt on a national scale. Researchers who are willing to listen sympathetically to their fellow human beings will be able to find abundant case reports. What is still unresolved, of course, is the meaning of the case material, and it is chiefly in this area that I hope that I have made some inroads.

In closing, I want to reemphasize that the statement I am making about the nature of these experiences (and, by extension, about others like them) is a very limited and specific one. To summarize: Many studies of supposed psychic phenomena dwell on the alleged peculiarities of perception and of cognition which typically attend them. For example, to consider the case of "apparitions" of the deceased, many investigators, both sympathetic and otherwise, focus their attention in such situations on the processes of sensory perceptions taking place in the person who reports observing the apparition. Sympathetic investigators try to establish that what was seen was in fact the spirit of the deceased; investigators bent on impugning the experience try to demonstrate that it was a "hallucination," *i.e.*, a product of a disordered nervous system.

Or, when the purported paranormal event involves someone appearing to "know" something which he or she was in no position to know, investigators of both schools of thought tend to pay attention almost exclusively to the cognitive processes involved. For example, numerous cases have been reported in which a person describes a precognitive experience. Perhaps he or she has a dream in which something occurs which he or she could not possibly have known in advance, and the prophecied event later transpires. Here sympathetic investigators argue for the existence of supernatural channels of knowledge, while skeptics retort that the happening came about through chance coincidence, or a "lucky guess."

In the final analysis, my own position does not coincide with either of the diametrically opposed points of view portrayed above. I do not mean to imply that such experiences are ultimately "real," nor that they are ultimately "unreal," *i.e.*, entirely hallucinatory or delusional.

Frankly, I do not know what the answer to this dilemma is.

I only wish to point out that, regardless of whether any such experiences are finally "real" or not, they frequently and regularly occur in the context of mourning and bereavement. Accordingly, it makes perfect sense to consider, when one is studying supposed psychic experiences, and to be sensitive *not only* to the apparent peculiarities of sensory perception and/or cognition with which they are associated, but also to the emotional context of human grief and bereavement in which they occur.

Finally, as I have also indicated, one cannot come to an understanding of these experiences without taking into account the fact that they involve a charismatic celebrity who was truly on a first-name basis with the whole world. He left his own unique imprint on them as he did on everything he touched. And in doing so, he managed to cast his spell over all of us and for all time.

Acknowledgments

Many people helped me in one way or another during the eight years that this volume was in preparation, and I want to express my appreciation to them all. First and foremost, I wish to thank the persons whose experiences are described in this book. I am grateful to them for allowing me to share their very personal feelings and impressions, and for listening with patience to my own preliminary and groping attempts to understand what had happened to them.

Numerous therapists, academicians, and researchers have taken time to relate to me stories of their own encounters with clients or subjects who had unusual psychic experiences involving Elvis Presley, and to share with me their own reflections or speculations on the psychodynamics involved in these most intriguing occurrences. I can publicly thank Dr. Bill Baldwin, Clyde Reid, Larry Scharwtz, and David Welthe. Others have requested and have been granted anonymity in order to protect the feelings and privacy of their clients, but I want them, too, to know how grateful I am for their sharing.

Robyn Quail helped in many ways: by referring me to new cases, by encouraging me to publish my findings, by guiding me to relevant literature, and by introducing me to her friend, Gail Brewer. Gail, in turn, shared some of her own fascinating experiences involving Elvis Presley and offered added encouragement. Bobby Smith kindly spent a long afternoon giving me a vivid account of his own firsthand observations of the behavior of whole crowds of people who tenaciously denied the reality of Elvis's death.

I am also indebted to Tim Hatcher, Jungian psychotherapist-in-training, for sharing with me his insightful reflections on Elvis as archetype. I have summarized and elaborated upon his observations in the concluding chapter of this book.

I want to convey my continuing gratitude, also, to John Egle of Mockingbird Books. He has listened patiently and with interest to my various ideas on this subject as they have developed over the past eight years. Thanks are due as well to Chuck Perry of Peachtree Publishers. When I first told him of this project, he responded with kindness, interest, and enthusiasm, all of which were most inspiring. And finally, Jeannette Feeney served as an excellent typist — always prompt, always accurate, always patient.

I hope that in the process of gathering and synthesizing the experiences, observations, and reflections of the many people whom I have thanked, I have succeeded in writing a book which would have been interesting and helpful to Elvis himself. It has been reported by those who were close to him that, especially during the later years of his life, Elvis also explored the realm of paranormal experience. No doubt his own spiritual search was motivated in part by a need to come to terms with the basis of his own enormous popularity. I would like to think that a book of this type would have helped him better to understand the amazing sway he held over so many of his fellow human beings.

About the Author

Raymond A. Moody, Jr., received the B.A., M.A., and Ph.D. from the University of Virginia. After teaching philosophy at East Carolina University, he received his M.D. from the Medical College of Georgia in 1976 and then served his residency at the University of Virginia Medical School. He is also the author of *Life After Life* and *Reflections on Life After Life.*